MW01518699

𝕿.𝕬.𝕻.

The Anointed Principles

The Journey To Unlock Spiritual Blessings

Shawn Morris

P.O. Box 1802

Alief, Texas 77411

prophet@shawnmorris.org

Please note that the capitalizes certain pronouns in scripture that refer to the Father, Son, and Holy Spirit, and may differ from some publishers' styles. Take note that the name satan and related names are not capitalized. We choose not to acknowledge him, even to the point of violating grammatical rules.

Unless otherwise noted, all Scripture quotations are from the King James Version of the Bible.

Scripture quotations marked "NKJV" are from the New King James Version of the Bible. Copyright © 1979, 1980, 1982 by Thomas Nelson, Inc., publishers. Used by permission.

English definitions are from *Webster's Pocket Dictionary and Thesaurus of the English Language,* new rev. ed. by V. Nichols, Nichols Publishing, 1999.

Biblical references are from *Zondervan's Compact Bible Dictionary* by T. Alton Bryant, Zondervan, 1994, and *Smith's Bible Dictionary* by William Smith, Nelson, 1964.

Hebrew and Greek definitions are from *The New Strong's Complete Dictionary of Bible Words* by James Strong, Nelson, 1996.

Copyright 2014 by Shawn Morris

Cover design and layout by [Exodus design].

ISBN: 0615895069
ISBN-13: 9780615895062

Foreword

Shawn is one of those unusual persons, who experience supernatural occurrences and manifestations of grace in their lives and ministries, because of the goodness of God and the presence of the Lord Jesus Christ. Through his desire to know the person of God the Father, he has been given the ability to receive divine revelations that bring about visible manifestations of the presence of Jesus in the now. As you read the pages of this book, your hunger for the Lord Jesus will be increased. Your thirst for the spirit and the anointing of God will be deepened, and your understanding of how to **T.A.P.** into the anointing of God will be sharpened. You will be able to experience Jesus in ways you never have before.

The revelation of the word that Shawn shares will enable you to see, hear, and know Jesus to the place where you can release the anointing and the power of God. As the light of God shines upon your spirit and soul, you will learn how to make Jesus known to others, and bring heaven to earth so others can experience both the love and the life of the living God. Jesus said, *"Unless you see signs and wonders, you will not believe"*. This **"show me generation"** must see signs, wonders, and miracles that are so profound in the natural that they will be led to genuine repentance, sincere faith, and deep intimacy with the Lord Jesus. Through *"The Anointed Principles of God"*, you will find information, inspiration, revelation, manifestation, and ultimate glorification of the Lord Jesus.

Dear follower of God, it is time for you to arise, and shine, for your light has come, and the glory of the Lord has risen upon you. Be prepared to enter into His light and His glory. As you read the pages of this book, may you know Jesus more intimately and manifest Him more evidently in your life and ministry. To God be the glory!

– Pastor Tony Kemp

President of Tony Kemp Ministrie
and Embassy Christian Center

Hannibal, Missouri

Endorsements

"T.A.P. is an interesting and thought provoking book. It will challenge your walk with God, open your eyes to the supernatural, and draw you to The Holy One. It contains Shawn Morris journey into the supernatural, as well as, principles that can change your life. Read it now, and start T.A.P'ing in to the power of God for your life."

– Joan Hunter

Author/Evangelist
President, Joan Hunter Ministries

"Shawn Morris's new book T.A.P. is an inspirational testimonial. T.A.P. will help the reader to T.A.P. in to the Kingdom."

– Kevin Basconi

Author/President,
King of Glory International Ministries

"If you are serious about the prophetic realm and want to understand how to live and operate in your prophetic gifting…then this is the book you need."

– Kathie Walters

Good News Ministries

"This is a great book on the anointing of God and how it operates. I highly recommend this written work of Prophet Shawn Morris, led of and totally anointed by the Holy Spirit. I totally endorse this book written by a mighty True Prophet of God. It has truly inspired my life…. This book is a must for this generation, and I would fully recommend it to all ministers of the Gospel. All churches should use this mighty book as a teaching aid for their classes. Prophet Shawn is a mighty man of prayer and moves in the anointing of the Holy Spirit; he is related to William J. Seymour of Azusa Street Revival. He is truly of a godly heritage. The power of God rules his life."

– Glenda Jackson

"If you really want to know someone, travel with them, especially in Israel. As I spent time with Prophet Shawn Morris on such a tour and in later meetings, I quickly saw he is the real deal. He walks what he talks and he talks what he walks. That's true integrity. In the book T.A.P., you meet the man who teaches with both his words and his actions. In this highly confessional work, you will see how each principle has been worked out in his life and his ministry. This book is a treasure trove of tried and true principles for walking and working in the glory of God. I know these principles will enrich your walk as you apply them in your spirit, soul, and body."

– James Durham

Author/Pastor/President
Higher Calling Ministries

"T.A.P. is a book that will help readers learn further in depth their identities in Christ and how to operate fully in the supernatural realm to advance the Kingdom of God on earth. I believe you will be richly blessed by the history and insight in this book."

– Munday Martin

Contagious Love International Ministries

Dedication

This

book

is

dedicated

to

"The Lost and the Suffering Body of Christ."

T.A.P!

Acknowledgments

First, I would love to acknowledge my God for ruling and reigning over my life. Second, I would love to honor and acknowledge Jesus Christ: my Lord, my Savior, my King, my Big Brother, my Friend, and my God, without you I never would have made it. Thank You once again for saving my soul. Third, I would love to honor one of the most important people in my life, one whom very few acknowledge. Yes, you, Holy Spirit. You're my Teacher, my Comforter, my Advisor, my tour guide through life, without You, I would be lost in this fallen world. Thank You for being the voice of reason in a realm of uncertainty.

To my wife, Tora: you are the most beautiful and anointed woman I have ever met. I thank God daily for bringing you into my life and into this ministry. When I found you, I knew I was a blessed man. Thank you for being my partner, my intercessor, my watchman, my soul mate, and my best friend. Thanks for motivating me and believing in me even when I didn't believe in myself. We are Bonnie and Clyde in the spirit realm. Love you always. Remember, we cannot lose.

To my children, Daniel, Ebony, Travis, Aracelis, Da'shawn, Ormini, Shanice, and Isaiah: I'll love you forever. You'll definitely keep me on my knees. Each one of you is destined for greatness.

"His seed shall be mighty upon the earth: generation of the upright shall be blessed." (Psalms 112:2). Thank you for being my inspiration.

A final acknowledgment goes out to my SMI family. I want to thank Evangelist JJ. Simmons for leading me to the Lord, and for pushing me to write this book. Thanks for being a lifetime friend and brother. See you at the top. To Justin and Rachael Eldred of AHOP Ministries for supporting this project: you are the best protégés any mentor could have. Love you guys always. Last but not least, I would like to acknowledge Angela Trippi for being a huge part of this ministry's success. Thanks for helping me type up and pre- edit the book. I thank God for sending me such a humble servant of Christ. Keep up the good work. This is just the beginning. We cannot lose!

– Prophet Shawn Morris

The Revival Encounter

The Avonshire Revival

The following historical event took place at a house church on the south west side of Houston, Texas. The event received no public attention, but it should have been written down in the history books as one of the greatest house revivals of modern times.

These true events took place in my living room at 13319 Avonshire Street in 2010. I had a burning desire for a revival to come to my city. I had no experience or education on the subject, so I started a journey to study and discover the recipe for a great awakening. My wife and I wanted more than just a Sunday routine week after week. We wanted God!

I started a Bible study in my house that gradually grew into a small house church. In the early days of the church meetings, all I would preach was repentance. The Lord used me often to prophesy over the people, and they would tell their friends to come see "this pastor who have told me about my whole life." The church grew to a good, solid twenty members. As long as I was prophesying, the people stayed.

But, when the Lord started telling me to preach on sin issues, church membership dwindled. One Sunday, no one showed up. It was just my wife, our children, and I. I was discouraged and devastated. I felt like I had let God and my family down. But my wife urged me to preach to her and the kids like they were the crowd. Even so, I needed new direction, and I needed it fast.

The Next Move

The church was dismantled, but I had to pull myself together. I made up my mind that God had promised me revival, and I wasn't going to stop seeking Him until I received it. I went on Sid Roth's *It's Supernatural!* website, and I found a show in his archives about the Azusa Street Revival. The author of the book was Tommy Welchel, and the name of the book was *"They Told Me Their Stories."* It was about the youth, who had been used by God at the Great Azusa Street Revival. I went to purchase the book on line from Sid Roth's website, but there were no more in stock.

I went to Tommy Welchel's website, and it directed me to buy the book from the printer. The name of the man who printed the book was Dr. J. Edward Morris. I found it ironic that we both shared the same last name. To top it off, he lived in Houston as well. I told the Lord, "You must be doing something here." Dr. Morris and I hit it off real well. We went out to lunch, and he took my wife and me to his house. He gave us two copies of the book. He kept insisting that I needed to write a book, but I just wanted to read about how they had ushered in a revival.

As I read the book, my faith sparked. I longed to see those kinds of miracles in my own life.

Answered Prayers

Several weeks passed, and I read the book over and over again. I would cry out at the altar in our living room for the Spirit to move like He did at Azusa Street. I told the Lord I didn't want the burden of revival if it wasn't like Azusa. I didn't even want to do the work of the ministry anymore if His presence didn't manifest.

We began to invite people out for our monthly revival meetings at the house. Many came since they didn't feel obligated to join our house church. In Houston, if you didn't have a building, then you weren't a church. One day, I was on a three day dry fast, no water and no food; we call it the "Esther fast." My wife was running last minute errands before the meeting. She left me alone in the house so I could seek the Lord.

I laid prostrate on the floor and tried to enter into the Holy of Holies. I started to fall asleep, and I heard a voice say, "Tonight revival is coming." I remained on the floor and saw visions of clouds; My eyes were closed, and my body went numb as I saw a bright light. All of a sudden, my wife walked in the door and said, "What have you done?"

I opened my eyes and said, "What did I do?" The house was full of a thick mist that covered the entire floor. I got up to see it clearly, and as soon as I raised my hand, my wife flew across the room. She fell every time I went near her. That night, I was waiting to see what would happen. I knew my wife had felt the power of God, but what about the people's reactions?

It was 7:00 p.m. on a Friday, and people began to come in. Some could barely see because of the cloud. Some were slain in the Spirit as they walked through the door. They were not hurt as they fell forward to the marble floor on their faces. I had seen people fall backward before, but never forward. It was all new to me. Many would fall from their chairs as I preached messages of repentance. Some couldn't get off the floor because their legs where weighed down by the Shekinah glory that filled the house.

For months, oil from heaven dripped from our ceiling in all our rooms. People wouldn't leave the meetings till four or five in the morning. Gold dust appeared inside and outside of the cars lining the street. Neighbors reported seeing a cloudy mist around our house at all times during the day. At some of the meetings, people said they saw rainbows and flashes of light by our pulpit. It would actually rain inside the house when we worshiped God.

People came from other cities to see the manifestation and movement of God at our little house church. Convictions were so heavy that homosexual men and women would get converted instantly and start speaking in tongues.

The Lord also used the youth to prophesy. My eleven year old daughter Ida would stand in front of people and call out accurate words of knowledge. Grown men and women would fall down and bursting into tears because of the accuracy. There were miracles of instant weight-loss, money appeared in bank accounts, purses, and wallets, and many miraculous healings and heavenly visitations took place. God visited us in powerful ways. My prayers had been answered. Revival had arrived!

The Fire Fades

The revival on Avonshire lasted about eight months, and no one understood how it came or how it went. The media never got involved, but those who were touched by it will never forget its impact. The landlord and the neighborhood association banned us from having meetings in the house. The AC unit and many other household appliances started to break down, and the oil that dripped from the ceiling dried up. It was over; The fire had faded, and any hopes of it spreading worldwide proved to be a pipe dream. During the revival, many prophets came and prophesied that we were carriers of revival. One said I had the mantle of William J. Seymour, not knowing that I had been studying about him prior to the Avonshire revival.

Prophetess Glenda Jackson, who is the niece of Maria Woodworth-Etta, told me that, one day, she was reading my book and God told her Prophet Shawn is the descendant of William J. Seymour of the Azusa Street Revival. She said the Lord told her that I carried the one-hundred year prophesy that was spoken by Seymour around 1910. She said revival would come out through my ministry to fulfill the prophecy of my ancestors. When Prophetess Glenda shared this with me, the Holy Spirit hit me like a lightning bolt. I was struck by the power of God; Waves of glory went through my body. Other prophets had said that to me before, but when this woman of God said it, the Lord confirmed the word with signs following. I saw why the Lord gave us such grace. I was a part of the revival blood-line of God's generals, just like Glenda. Even though the Avonshire revival wasn't on the level of Azusa Street, the Holy Spirit graced us with a taste of what's to come. If the Lord had allowed me to experience that measure of His Spirit at Avonshire when I was spiritually immature, imagine what would happen in the days to come as we began to T.A.P. into the wells of revival.

Lord, I pray that you pour out your Spirit in great measure. Open up the closed wells of the revival of our ancestors, and send water to a dry and thirsty land. Send conviction to the lost sheep, and help us turn from our wicked ways. Allow the prophecy of God's general, William J. Seymour, to come to pass now! We receive revival, renewal, restructure, restoration, and awakening in Jesus name.

Table of Contents

Introduction

What is T.A.P.?

Let's break down the meaning of T.A.P.

T.A.P. stands for **"The Anointed Principles"** of God. Let's start off by defining what the anointing or anointed is. "Anointed" is a translation of the Hebrew word *mishchah,* which means "unction" or "gift." There is a misconception of the anointing and the glory. The anointing is a gift of God's glory or unction to move in His glory. "Unction" is translated from the Greek word *charisma,* which means "special endowment of the Holy Spirit."

You may ask what an endowment is. Well, to endow is to supply with a permanent income or income producing property or to bestow upon. Anointing is an investment or endowment from the Lord that constantly produces income. As we work for the Lord, we will see a resulting increase. We work *for* the Lord, and *with* the Lord, to produce fruit in the earthly realm.

Let's go to Matthew 25:14–15:

> *"For the kingdom of heaven is as a man traveling into a far country, who called his own servants, and delivered unto them his goods. And unto one he gave **five** talents, to another **two**, and to another **one**; to every man according*

to his several abilities; and straightway took his journey."
[Emphasis added]

In this parable, Jesus explains how different people receive different measures, or amounts, of the anointing. A lot of people think we all have the same level of anointing, or gifts and talents. Case in point: Ephesians 4:8 says, *"Wherefore he saith. When he ascended up on high, he led the captivity captive, and **gave gifts** unto men"* (emphasis added). Then, if you scroll down to verse eleven, it lists the gifts He gave: *"And he gave some apostles; and some prophets; and some evangelists and some, pastors and teachers"* (Ephesians 4:11). Notice that the writer used the word *some*, not *all*. Also notice he named five gifts, just like the five talents Jesus mentioned in Matthew 25:15: *"And unto one he gave **five talents**, to another two, and to another one; to every man according to his several abilities."* (emphasis added). The biblical meaning of the number five is grace, the enabling power of God. I believe the five talents in this parable represent the five-fold ministry of Jesus that Paul wrote about in Ephesians 4:8–11.

But, like it says in Matthew 25:15, it was *"according to his several abilities."* What's ability? Ability means possessing the necessary qualities to carry out an action. It can also mean "competence, skill, or a particular talent." Wow! So this coincides with the parable of the talents. Everyone doesn't have the same talent or gift; some can move in all five, some in two, and some in only one. But, we are all given *some* gift or talent to produce more income for the Lord.

Remember, the Lord gave us these gifts for the profit of all, so He may get returns on His investments. The anointing is God's currency with man. That is why in Matthew 25:18, Jesus said: *"But he that had received one went and dug in the earth, and hid his lord's money [gift or talent]."* God knows who will be good stewards or investors of His anointing. So, if you are lacking in the anointing, it's very likely you need to increase your investment skills.

How do we increase our investment skills? Well, I am glad you asked. The last letter in T.A.P. stands for **"principles."** One meaning of the word principle, translated from the Greek word *arche*, which is "first in rank, first in time." God is no respecter of persons, but He is a respecter of principles. When it comes to the anointing, you have majors and minors just like in college. But we have a lot of people majoring in their minors and minoring in their majors. We have pastors trying to be prophets and prophets trying to be pastors. We wonder why they are not receiving the fullness of God. It is because they are out of position or out of rank.

Another meaning of *principle* is a "fundamental law or truth upon which others are based; a moral standard." When something is fundamental, it is of major significance and the primary origin of everything that springs from it. Principles are significant to your Christian walk. When you follow God's principles, then you can find the **"Prince"** in the principle. The Lord shows us who He is through His attributes. If we follow the principles outlined in this book, we can obtain every promise and possess every gift, talent, and anointing God has in store for those who are good stewards. So let's get ready to T.A.P.!

Chapter 1
Glory Chasers

What is "glory"? The words translated as *"glory"* in our English Bible comes from several Hebrew and Greek words with various meanings. For instance, a lot of people are familiar with the Hebrew word **kaboud**, which means "splendor," "honor," "reverence," or "glory." Another Hebrew word, **tohar**, means "brightness," "purification" or "glory." The Greek word **kleo** means "renown," "honor," or "glory." All of these words have been translated as *"glory"* in various places in the Bible. I will not discuss the difference between the anointing and the glory in this book. However, I will emphasize the importance of the anointing, and its role in accessing the glory realm.

I decided I wanted all the different facets of God's glory. The Hebrew word **Shekinah** is not in the Bible, but is used in Jewish theology to refer to the presence of God and is also found in the Targums writings. When coupled with glory, Shekinah refers to the tangible or visible presence of God. I knew that was what I needed, so the hunt was on. Since this was all new to me, I had to become a student of those who moved in the glory. I had to start at the beginning and work my way up. I had to get a "master's degree" in the anointing before I could become a glory chaser. The only person I knew at the time who talked about the anointing was

1

Benny Hinn. So I started to desire and pray to meet him. Here we go let's T.A.P.!

My First Encounter with Benny

When I first got saved, all I wanted people to do was repent. Since I didn't have a church home or a pastor, my friend Joel and I started our own Bible studies in our apartment complex. We would watch TBN or Daystar programs on television and listen to well known preachers for information. But we had no revelation about how to do what they were doing.

We were particularly drawn to Benny Hinn. At first I thought his anointing was fake, but for some reason, I still wanted what he had. I read several of his books, the one that helped me the most was "*Good Morning, Holy Spirit.*" I knew my life would be different if I could encounter the Holy Spirit like Pastor Benny.

I first encountered Pastor Benny in the spirit through a night vision. In my dream, Pastor Benny and I were in a boat, floating down a creek. To my left, I saw the church I was attending at the time. The land was beautiful, and the church I attend looked like the United States' White House in Washington, DC. I saw my wife at the time, and the church members, they where gesturing for me to come join them. All of a sudden, Pastor Benny screamed at me with a stern voice, "*Don't you listen to those people! You will build God's church in the water.*" Then I woke up.

At first I was puzzled by my dream. Later on, the Holy Spirit explained to me that the church I was attending had its foundation on land, where it was easy to build. He said my ministry would be built on the emphasis of the Holy Spirit, which is what the water represented. That dream has come to pass, and I know it was God who sent the initial warning to me through Pastor Benny.

The Prophetic Calling

Let me give you the history of my calling before my destiny was unlocked. When I was born again, I decided to try to reconcile with my wife, but the past hurt from both parties were too great. She was a prophetess, who heard from God. She was a gifted seer and loved the Lord, but she also had a bad temper and a filthy mouth. We both had a low level of respect for one another. The love in the relationship had diminished completely. So, we began our attempt at reconciliation by going to church together. I really loved the church and the people. They were from my home city, and the pastor was really down to earth. His wife was a powerful woman of God who moved heavily in the gift of prophecy and intercession, as did all the women in the church. Before my arrival at the church, I'd only heard of other prophets. However, I'd never seen anyone else use the gift consistently except for my wife.

Before I was saved, my wife would go to their meetings and lay my picture on the altar. They would all travail for my salvation. So, when I got saved, it was a miracle. One day, the pastor's wife told me, God had called me to be a prophet. I was skeptical about prophets because of what my wife used to say about the calling. I thought I wasn't qualified. I thought I had to be born a prophet, with a halo over my head.

This woman of God proceeded to tell me that "God is not looking for celebrities; He is looking for servants." But, she said, "since you are a servant, He will make you a celebrity." From that day, I pursued my prophetic calling in spite of what my wife or others said. I had to

3

convince myself this was the will of God for my life. When you receive a prophetic word, you must digest it thoroughly; you eat the fish and spit out the bones. Let no one deter you from pursuing your calling. Jealousy and envy will rise up, and the enemy will try to torment you daily about your assignment. I want to encourage you to stay diligent as you chase the glory, because there is a silver lining around every cloud.

The Stage Is Set

Joel called me one day and said, "Bro! Benny Hinn is in town!" I asked, "Where?" He told me he was going to be at Saint Agnes's Church in Houston. So I told Joel that my wife and I would go.

When we arrived, the church was packed with five thousand people in two different buildings. Unfortunately, our seats were in the second building. There, we watched a live stream of the event happening in the main building. All of a sudden, my wife started getting sleepy and sick. I didn't want to leave, even though my only choice was to watch Benny Hinn on a screen.

Several hours passed, and I started to grow weary as well. Yet, something kept telling me to stay in spite of my wife's pleas to go home. Then, it was announced that Benny Hinn was coming to the second building where we were. The crowd went crazy! When he came in, it was still too packed to get to the front where he was.

Then Benny said, "I want all ministers and pastors to come to the front." Trying to be a good husband and stay with my ailing wife, I didn't go. All of a sudden I heard a voice say, "Go! Now!" So I went forward but the crowd was still too big for me to reach the front.

Then I heard Benny say, "You! Come here!" Everyone looked around, and so did I. He was pointing directly at me! My heart began to race. I

4

had prayed for this for months, but I had no idea what was about to take place. Time slowed down, and everything from that point on progressed in slow motion. I didn't know what was about to happen, but I knew for sure that this was a kairos moment being written in the heavens.

The Prophetic Word

Once I was on stage, Benny looked at me and waved his hand. All of a sudden, I felt like a strong wind had hit me; My legs became weak, I hit the floor, and I started to weep uncontrollably. Then I heard him call someone to come on stage to pick me up. When I looked up, Joel was standing over me. Benny had called him out of a crowd of about five thousand to come and pick me up. Out of excitement Joel kept saying, "Dog! Benny Hinn! Dog! Benny Hinn!"

They picked me up, then Benny waved his hand, and I hit the floor again. He then stood over me and said, "This man has a great anointing on his life, let me tell you, he will do what I do." I couldn't believe what he had just said. Someone like me to do what Benny Hinn does? No way! I was happy with just meeting him and experiencing what I later learned was getting slain in the spirit. When I got up, I felt different but still didn't understand the full concept of it. I had received many prophecies in the past, but this was different not because it was Benny Hinn but because I felt a tangible touch. My wife at the time didn't want to admit it, but she knew from that day forward, that I was chosen by God to do great exploits for His Kingdom.

Did I Really Receive?

A couple of days went by, and the excitement started to wane. I wondered if I had actually received something, or if Benny had just spoken encouraging words to me. One thing I knew for sure was that I was slain in the spirit. Replicating what Benny said seemed a little far out there. There was no way I could do what he did. I couldn't understand it at all. So, I began to go into deep prayer about it. I closed my eyes tight, and I started to pray until I felt relaxed. I started to feel light. I raised my hands to my face, and to my shock, both of my hands were engulfed in blue flames! I was alarmed, but not afraid. I knew it was from God. This wasn't just a vision, flames that I could see with my natural eyes, were actually on my hands. The flames were an electric blue color, like lightning, but brighter. I didn't know what was taking place, but it was heavenly. That was my first time seeing in the spirit realm, and it was amazing.

Understanding the Vision

As I looked, the blue flames on my hands disappeared. But something unusual was still there. My hands were hot, and I mean burning hot, but not enough to hurt me. Several days later I asked people at my church what was going on with my hands, but no one had an answer. I thought I might have arthritis or carpal tunnel syndrome. I didn't know what to do.

One day I ran into a pastor and told him what had happened with Benny Hinn and the blue flames on my hands. He told me, "Brother Shawn, God has given you the healing anointing." He let me know that people like William Branham, Oral Roberts, A.A. Alan, and John G. Lake felt burning sensations in their hands when they ministered under this healing anointing. From that point on I understood what I had received. Now that I know how to T.A.P. and receive a gift, talent, or anointing, I now desire the same for you. Let's finish the journey.

Now What?

I had just received this wonderful gift from the man of God. When I told people, they would tell me that God gets all the credit, man does not get any glory. I understood God gets the glory; but I wondered why, I hadn't received this gift until the man of God laid hands on me? Then I saw in Scripture: "***Neglect not the gift*** *that is* ***in you,*** *which* ***was given to you by prophecy,*** *with the* ***laying on the hands*** *of the* ***eldership***" (1 Timothy 4:14). That's what Pastor Benny did with me; he prophesied and then laid his hands on me as an elder in the faith. It wasn't until a man laid hands, then the gift was release to me. Before this encounter I had no knowledge or experience about the gifts of the spirit, until that impartation from Pastor Benny. But, just like the Scripture says, I shouldn't neglect the gift. To neglect something means to ignore it or fail to perform it. I was in a church that didn't allow me to operate in those gifts unless I was either commissioned by the pastors or bishop, or properly ordained. In other words, I had to go through the proper protocol. Unfortunately, to follow the protocol of my church, I had to neglect my gift.

Faithful but Dying

I was faithful to my church and my pastor. He was a real man of God. He taught me the moral standards I needed to be a real man, as well as a man of God. But my desire for more of the Holy Spirit was eating me alive. Also, my marriage was failing. I knew this was not God's best. I told the Lord, He might as well keep me in the world, rather than have me suffer like this trying to serve Him. I said to Him, "I want your best or nothing at all."

My church family urged me to be patient and stay humble, but it's hard to stay patient when you're hungry for more of God. So, I asked the Lord to let my zeal line up with His will. The church had a "minister in training" class that I took, but I saw no demonstration of God's power like I had seen with Benny Hinn or like what I read in Scripture about Jesus. At that time, the biggest demonstration of the Spirit that flowed through my church was prophecy, and that seemed elementary to me even though I never did it myself.

I was at war between my faithfulness to the church and my obedience to God. Something had to give because I was dying on the vine. Many believers are more obligated to their church than they are to God's assignment for their lives. The man pleasing spirit has kept many from speaking God's truth and moving to the next level in their walk out of fear of man's disproval. We must not be limited to man's opinion, we must obtain God's unlimited supply of favor for our obedience to Him, not man.

Breaking the Soul Ties

By this time, I was in charge of the evangelistic team at my church. Rumors about me traveling to other churches started surfacing. I used to take trips to see Benny Hinn whenever he was close to my region. That was totally against my church's protocol. They felt you had to be faithful to your own church and not get fed from others.

Then one day I heard that voice again, the same voice I had heard at Benny Hinn's service telling me, "Go! Now!" But this time it said, "*This marriage grieves me.*" So I started binding and loosing and pleading the blood of Jesus over my marriage. But the voice continued to say the same thing. It seemed like my marriage was over; we only stayed together because of ministry. The doctrine of our church was that divorce was against the will of God. If I were to leave the marriage, I would be outside of His perfect will.

I told Joel about what had happened, and he told me that was in Scripture. He said to go to Ephesians 4:30–32:

> *"And* **grieve not the Holy Spirit of God**, *whereby ye are sealed unto the day of redemption. Let* **all bitterness**, *and* **wrath**, *and* **anger**, *and* **clamour**, *and* **evil speaking**, *be put away from you, with all malice. And* **be kind** *one to one another,* **tenderhearted, forgiving one another**, *even as God for Christ's sake hath forgiven you." [Emphasis added]*

Wow! It was right there in Scripture! My wife and I were definitely not kind or tenderhearted to one another. We had bitterness, anger, un-forgiveness, etc. But I still wasn't sure what to do because of what my church was saying. I thought I must not have been hearing from God. One day I stumbled upon the Scripture that said, *"For what knowest thou, O wife, whether thou shalt save thy husband? Or how knowest thou, O man, whether thou shalt save thy wife?"* (1 Corinthians 7: 16). That was it! God didn't like divorce, but he didn't believe in bad marriages either.

I counsel married couples across the country, and I see anointed women of God who stay in bad marriages that God did not ordain. So many stay in abusive and violent relationships because they are under this false doctrine that tells them, life is over if they get a divorce. When my divorce was finalized, the Lord told me clearly, "If I forgave you for the crimes you committed, I'll forgive you for breaking covenant."

Now, don't misunderstand me, I am not promoting divorce. However, most people who are connected with unbelievers think just because they are saved, their spouse will automatically get saved. That's why the Scripture says, *"Do not yoke up with unbelievers."* Many believers try to play the role of the Holy Spirit for their spouses. They meet in the flesh and try to convert unholy relation-ships into holy covenants. Now, my wife and I were both believers at the time, but because of my past and her lack of respect, we were both unbelievers, not in Christ, but in the marriage itself. We can be believers in God, and not be believers in one another or the covenant we're under. One day I was in a meeting in Dallas/Fort Worth, Texas, with Dr. Mike Murdock. He looked me in the eyes, and he quoted these prophetic words: "Go where you're celebrat-ed, not where you are tolerated." That day I received my identity back. I put it in my heart that I would no longer be disrespected, because I realized I was a king.

Allow me to share a Rhema word that will keep you from mak-ing the same mistakes I did. Here is a revelation the Lord gave to me about Godly marriages. The Scriptures say, *"He who findeth a wife findeth a good thing, and obtained favor of the Lord."*

One: *"he who findeth."* First of all, the man find the wife, not God. Most people expect God to play match maker for them, and the truth of the matter is, it's our job to find our mates. The Lord will give you instruction on what kind of mate to look for, but it's up to you to pick, like Abraham's servant did for Isaac.

The Lord told me that *"He who findeth,"* pertains to a man un-der a Godly covenant. Ladies, when you meet a man and he is not fully persuaded about his walk with God, don't marry him. I tell the ladies in our ministry, if a man is not speaking in tongues at one hundred miles per hour, don't even give him the time of day. They say, "Prophet, why?" I tell them, "Because if he is not full of the Spirit, he will fulfill the lust of the flesh." If a man is not faithful to God, he won't be faithful to you.

A lot of women claim to be a "Proverbs 31" type of woman but lack the scriptural reference. First a "Proverbs 31" woman was a married woman, so if you're not married this does not apply to you.

Second a "Proverbs 31" woman's husband must be a well-known man of God. Verse 23 of that chapter says, *"Her husband is known in the gates, when he sitteth among the elders of the land."* If your husband is not a well-known and respected man of God then you're not "Proverbs 31."

Another thing ladies, is that he must find you; it is not your job to find him. When you meet a man, don't display your Christianity card upfront. Let him do the talking, and then later on you expose your hand. Sorry guys.

Two: *"findeth a good thing."* Guys, this is where you come in. When you are looking for a bride, she must also be a woman of God. Proverbs 31:30 says, *"Favor is deceitful, and beauty is vain: but a woman that feareth the Lord, she shall be praised."* If you have a wife who does not fear the Lord, then she won't respect you. She must be a good thing, not a drama queen or Mrs. Attitude, but a kind and gentle soul. The Scriptures say in Proverbs 21:19, *"It is better to dwell in the wilderness, than with a contentious and an angry woman."* The Lord would rather we live in the jungle than deal with a crazy, hot tempered man or woman.

Three: *"and obtained favor of the Lord."* If you're not obtaining favor in your marriage then that's probably not your spouse. After the first two principles are applied, God will release favor upon your marital covenant.

There are several reasons why God would decide not to release favor on your marriage. The first is found in Titus 2:5. This is a description of how a wife should be: *"To be discreet, chaste, keepers at home, good, **obedient to their own husbands, that the word of God*** *be not blasphemed.*" (emphasis added). A lack of obedience and respect from a wife towards her husband will cause God's word to be nullified in the home, and give satan authorization to attack. The second one is found in 1 Peter 3:7: "*Likewise, ye husbands, dwell with them according to knowledge, **giving honour unto the wife,** as unto the weaker vessel, and **together** of the grace of life; **that your prayers be not hindered.**"* (emphasis added). The lack of honor and respect you show to your wife will hinder your prayer life, and once again, satan will have access to your health, happiness, and finances. Both parties must never take one another for granted. You are in a partnership for life, and both individuals are necessary.

I hope this helped someone. This wasn't supposed to make the book, but the Spirit of God said differently. I pray, in the name of Jesus Christ, that you break the ungodly soul ties and step into a Godly, Jesus sanctified, covenant relationship. In the words of Dr. Mike Murdock, go where you're celebrated, not where you're tolerated. T.A.P.

My Time Was Up

After I heard the voice, a few weeks passed. One day I was going to work, and the same voice said, "Full-time ministry."

I said to myself, "I know that is not God. I can barely pay the rent with the two jobs I have." I was working with my pastor on a FedEx truck delivering packages and at Popeye's as a cook. So, I told the voice, "If this is really you, God show me!"

And the voice responded, "I will."

That Monday I got on the truck with my pastor as usual to make deliveries. He told me that FedEx was conducting deep background checks on all employees, including helpers, so he was going to have to let me go. I was devastated; how was I going to face my wife and tell her, I was going to have to depend on Popeye's as my main source of income? But she didn't care. She told me she was leaving me, as soon as, she got her income tax return. I was devastated. I didn't know what to do or where to go. Everyone I knew was in New Orleans. I didn't want to return there because I knew God had called me to Houston.

I tried to get the pastor to give us a counseling session, but my wife told him she didn't want to be with me anymore. The physical abuse between my wife and I became so unbearable, that I resorted to sleeping in my van and taking showers at the gym where I had a membership. The pastor tried his best to keep it a secret because we both had leadership positions in the church. But one day, my wife stole the van from me while I was on a job interview. I had to walk several miles to the church to get my van. I stormed into the church in a rage, and my wife and I began to physically fight in the pastor's office before service. The whole church heard the altercation. When the fight was broken up, my wife gave me an evil smile and whispered, "I got you." She'd set me up for embarrassment in front of the pastor and his wife. I was humiliated. I knew my reputation in the church would only diminish from that day forward. My time was up.

The Last Straw

It seemed as if things couldn't get any worse. I was going to work at Popeye's when the voice showed up again and said, "I told you full-time ministry."

Again I said, "Show me!"

Again, the voice replied, "I will."

As soon as I entered my work place that evening, I discovered that my name was missing from the weekly schedule. They told me they were training new employees from another store and would call me if they needed me. So I said, "Okay! I got it now!"

Joel told me, "Brother, why don't you sell your Christian rap songs on the streets to pay your bills?"

I responded, "Amen! That is a good idea!" So I pressed fifty CDs and announced to my pastor and the church that I was going into full-time ministry. There was silence in the sanctuary.

The pastor looked up at the congregation and said, "I know some of y'all don't understand what the brother is doing, but we're going to support him anyway. One day you might see him here, and the next day on TV somewhere." Without realizing it the pastor was prophesying my exit out of the church and my entrance into building the Kingdom. God equips us for the work of ministry, not the work of the church (see Ephesians 4:12). I felt I was being pulled further and further away from the church. Even my pastor, who I looked up to as a big brother and spiritual father, seemed distant to me.

This succession of events made me give up on convincing the church that I was loyal, and on reconciling with my spouse. I thought I would have gained more support from my church, but I didn't. It seemed as if they took her side more than mine, because she had been with them longer, plus she was a woman. I was just a newly converted husband. They knew of her quick temper but excused it with Scriptures, saying she was a weaker vessel. Basically they told me I should have been able to take the abuse because I am a man. However, the verbal abuse was just as bad as the physical abuse. I knew the latest incident at the church was the last straw; I was finished.

This Is My Voice

There was a Wal-mart across the street from the apartment complex where my wife and I lived. She was so sick of my presence that she would walk into the other room when I came inside. She showed no signs of moving out, despite her constantly telling me that she was leaving. At the time, she was the only one working because I had just lost both jobs. So, I decided to go into full-time ministry. This was a language the church and she did not understand. She kept stressing that she wanted me gone. I knew it wouldn't be long before she kicked me out the house again. So, to pay my bills, I decided to sell my gospel rap CD's in front of the Wal-mart across the street. I was not a very good street salesman. One day I had made only three dollars in CD sales. Then that voice came to me and said, "*Go to the bathroom and pray.*" So I walked into the store and went to the restroom to pray.

All of a sudden, a guy walked in, and the voice said, "Pray for James."

So I turned to the guy and said, "Sir, I know you don't know me. But God just told me to pray for James."

He looked at me with a surprised expression on his face and replied, "James? I am James."

Then cold chills rushed through my body. I told him everything about his life and family. He fell on his knees in the bathroom and gave his life to Jesus. We both walked out of the restroom crying. People gave us weird looks. After all, we were two grown men coming out of the bathroom weeping. It was the Holy Spirit who had told me to pray for James. If I had not obeyed and opened my mouth, James would not have received salvation that day. The voice I now knew to be the Holy Spirit, said, "*From now on, when*

15

you hear this voice, you know this is me speaking to you." At that point, I knew God was with me. I now had a true calling on my life.

A Visitation for the Nations

It was wintertime and I had finally left my wife, and was now sleeping from house to house. One night I had an encounter. It wasn't a mere dream it was a visitation. In it, I was arguing with my now ex-wife in front of hospital doors. I had two suitcases with me. I told her, "Are you coming with me, or you staying at the hospital?" She told me she was going to stay. So, I took my suitcases and stood in front of a bus stop. This huge Greyhound looking bus pulled up. I got on and realized I was the only one on the bus. I was afraid because I had seen something like this in a horror movie. I yelled out to the bus driver, "Where are you taking me?"

When the bus driver turned around and took off his hat, he had a crown of thorns on his head. I saw his eyes and blood streaming down his face. It was Jesus!

When I woke up, I was pale as a ghost; I am a dark skinned guy, but I was as white as snow at that moment.

The Interpretation of the Visitation

When I told people about my visitation, they would get goose bumps all over and become drunk in the spirit. In the week following the visitation, I went to a prophetic church and stood in line for prayer. The pastor prayed for everyone. When he came to me, he paused and looked at me. He said, "He is giving you His eyes."

Immediately the encounter flashed before my eyes, and I was slain in the spirit. I asked a few people who knew how to interpret dreams and visions, and this was their interpretation: The hospital my wife and I were in front of represented the church. The suitcases indicated I was about to travel. The bus represented the size of my ministry. And the visitation also let me know that I was leaving my wife and the church to pursue my ministry with the Lord. The part about showing me His eyes was to let me know what kind of ministry I would have. The eyes represented the seer and the prophetic anointing. The blood dripping was to let me know that I needed to live a sacrificial lifestyle and suffer for His name sake in order to receive and maintain that anointing.

That prophesy in the vision came to pass. I now travel across the world preaching, prophesying, and laying hands on the sick and they recover with signs following. Imagine if I wouldn't have stepped out on faith to chase after the glory of God. I wouldn't be writing to you today. Follow the Lord and T.A.P.!

Discovering My Destiny

Now, to the good parts of the glory chasers saga. By that time my wife had left me, and I was homeless. I didn't have a job, and I couldn't afford an apartment because full-time ministry wasn't generating enough income. I slept at the homes of several of my church friends. Being a man of God who was going through a divorce was not a popular mark to have in the church world. The warm welcomes I received were short lived. A spirit of lust and perversion tried to attach itself to me. I was vulnerable without a wife, job, place to live, or family in Texas. I hit rock bottom.

It was 2010. I told the Lord that if He had allowed me to prophesy that the New Orleans Saints football were going to the Super

Bowl, which they did go, and they took home the title. Then I could also prophesy my future through a petition. I wrote a list of ten things I wanted for 2010. Just to name a few, I wrote that I wanted a divorce and I wanted a new wife. My new wife had to be beautiful, from another country, and supportive of my ministry. I wanted a great anointing, to travel, to get ordained as a pastor in the five-fold ministry, etc. Within five months I was divorced, and I met my new beautiful wife, Adetoro Peju Adegbenro, we call her Tora for short. Her family is from Nigeria.

I was young in the faith, and no one would ordain me, so I began to preach at my house and built up a small congregation. I wasn't looking to start a church. However, the people felt they needed my spiritual leadership. So, I decided I needed the proper licensing and credentials to pastor a church. Because I was young in the faith, and lacked affiliation with a clergy and proper mentorship, many refused to ordain me even though they saw God working through me. But one day, God came to the bishops in their dreams who told me I needed to be seasoned. He told them to ordain the prophet (me) as a pastor in the five-fold ministry. See, when you have a destiny nothing can forfeit your success.

Then the Lord told me, "If I've answered eight out of ten, what makes you think I won't answer the other two?" I had finally found a way to T.A.P. into my breakthrough. Now it was time to teach others.

I Love Lucy

I was in Dallas for a revival led by a pastor I knew. The pastor had guest speakers coming from out of town, Sito and Lucy Rael. I was only used to the ministers I saw on Christian television. I'd heard about this glory business for several months. I'd seen YouTube clips of people like Joshua Mills who'd witnessed manifestations of gold dust, but I wasn't quite sure if this stuff was real or not. I wanted the glory, but I didn't really know what I was asking for.

I sat in the third row of this meeting. I watched gold dust fall from the pages of Lucy Rael's Bible as oil dripped from her hands. The icing on the cake was when blood started to flow out of her hand like the crucifixion of Jesus. I said to my friend, "This lady is a witch or this is all staged."

Then, she walked down the aisles and spoke words of knowledge over the people. At first, she passed me by, but then she backtracked to me and said, "You're God's prophet, and don't question anymore who you are." It was confirmation of the call I'd heard all along. All of a sudden thick gold dust appeared in my hand, and the whole crowd started taking pictures. Lucy did lay hands on me, but only on my shoulder. I had finally T.A.P.ed into what I was missing.

Later, when I returned to Houston, heavy gold dust started manifesting at our meetings. I asked the Lord to show me a Scripture that confirmed the gold dust manifestations were from Him. He gave me Job 28:6 : "*The stones of it are the place of sapphires: and it hath dust of gold.*" (emphasis added). Wow! It was right there in Scripture. Sister Lucy introduced me to the glory in a way I had never experienced. I knew then that the best was yet to come: T.A.P.!

Encounters in the glory

I finally started to understand my journey. I knew God had a plan for my life, and His existence was more real than I could have imagined.

One day Reinhard Bonnke, a healing evangelist from Africa had an impartation service in the United States. He was scheduled to be in Houston for a three day event. My wife Tora and I decided to go since we had no personal mentor. We decided we were going to get all we could from God by any means. We adopted a baby boy named Isaiah, whose mother was incarcerated. The child had two small tumors, one on his eye and one under his tongue the size of a nickel. Isaiah was only several weeks old when he was due for surgery to remove the tumors. My wife turned to me and said; "Baby, I believe if you pray for him he will be healed."

I agreed. I took baby Isaiah and lifted him up in the air, proclaimed his healing, and blew on him. The baby began to throw up. Fifteen minutes later as we were leaving for the meeting we checked the baby, and the tumor on his eye was gone. It had totally disappeared, but the one under his tongue was still there. I told my wife as we walked out the door, "Don't worry when we come back, the other one will be gone."

We finally arrived at the service, and it was packed with more than several hundred people. We had the privilege of sitting in the pastor's section of the meeting. To my surprise there came a Korean pastor being rolled in a wheelchair by his wife. They sat next to us. Several African pastors tried to pray for him, but to no avail.

All of a sudden, I heard the voice of God say, "*Pull him out of the chair.*" I did my best to ignore His voice. I began to reason with the Lord, explaining to Him how I hadn't been fasting and praying.

The Lord politely repeated, "*Pull him out of the chair.*"

So I decided to ask the pastor's wife if I could pray for her husband, hoping she would say no. She agreed to allow me to pray for him, so I began to lift him out the wheelchair. His wife suddenly said, "What are you doing?"

I told her, "Just trust me," and I started to walk with the pastor, holding him by his waist for support.

Then I heard the Holy Spirit say, "*Let him go*," so I did. At first his legs wobbled, then all of sudden, he started to walk on his own.

The crowd went crazy. Bodyguards rushed me because of the pandemonium. They said, "What are you doing?"

I replied, "I am just doing what Reinhard would do."

Then the event host said, "Let him go, and let him pray for the people."

As I prayed, people were touched by God. It was glorious. Afterwards, people came up to Tora and I and asked to take pictures with us. That was how word of our ministry in Houston spread, to God be the glory. To top it off, when we arrived home, the tumor under baby Isaiah's tongue had completely disappeared just as I had spoken it. It was a miracle! Now we didn't have to put this newborn baby through surgery. We thank God often for that miracle.

Here are a few more encounters in the glory. I can't list them all because it would take up the whole book. So, let's begin.

There was a three day revival meeting in New Orleans, Louisiana. This was my hometown, and we knew that a prophet would not find respect in his own home or city. We arrived in New Orleans, and from the first day of the meeting opposition was evident. The event organizer backed out at the last minute, so we didn't have a venue for the meeting. Thankfully, a pastor friend of my sister allowed us to use his church. On the first night of the meeting, very few people showed up, and no manifestations took place. I was discouraged. My wife encouraged me that night after the service and said; "Baby, God didn't bring us out here for nothing." He will show up."

The next night more people showed up, including many of my family members. When I saw my family I was even more desperate for God to show himself. I knew this was an opportunity for the enemy to make me look false in front of them. The service started, and as I held an altar call, my grandma's pants started to fall. She experienced instantaneous weight-loss. Then, a lady jumped up to her feet, shouting that she'd just seen money appear in her purse. I'd seen miracles like these in Houston before, but I thought God would have to come down from His throne, in order for miracles to happen in a city like New Orleans. These signs and wonders were great, but I knew it would take more than falling pants and money appearing to convince my family.

Without warning, a woman, whose husband had run her over just moments earlier, crawled into the sanctuary. She was bleeding from various wounds and tears in her flesh, and her arm was broken. To top it off, she had a heavy drug smell on her from using crack cocaine. When the pastor saw her, he called for me and said, "Prophet, please help this lady." I went over to pray for her, and I told the people to help stand her up.

What you are about to hear next is a miracle. I've never seen anything like it since. All of a sudden, the lady started to stare into my eyes like she saw something or someone. Her arms popped and straightened out. The skin around her wounds grew back to its original color, as we looked at her. She then spoke in fluent tongues, and the crack cocaine smell disappeared. She was fully restored.

My family freaked out and backed away from me. From that day forward, some of my family members have feared talking to me. Some of them thought I was involved in witchcraft or voodoo. However, we knew it was the power of God that healed that lady and set her free from her bondage. Thank you Lord Jesus. Now that's what I call a miracle.

I will tell you about one more encounter I had while chasing the glory. I would like to tell you more, but I would need to write five more books just to cover it all. Any way let's continue, shall we?

A friend's church was having a grand opening, my wife and I decided to pay a visit. The pastor's wife held an altar call and asked the people who desired a touch from God to come up front. She asked my wife and I to come and pray for the people. We started to pray, and in came a woman with a walker who'd been paralyzed by a stroke. I prayed for her, and right before our eyes, the woman straightened out her arms and legs and ran around the church. My wife, Tora prayed for the piano player, and he fell under the power of God. Revival broke out, and the teenagers in the room started to cry for no reason. The power of God is always recognizable when the youth are touched. Today's youth will not fake it, or do courtesy drops, or show their emotions, unless it is real. In that service the youth were touched just as much as the adults.

There was a woman with a contracted arm, no blood circulated to the affected area of her body. Her doctors were scheduled to perform an amputation surgery the following week. After she saw the paralyzed woman receive her miracle, she was emboldened in her faith, and wanted to receive her own miracle. By the grace and glory of God, her arm loosened and straightened out. She regained full use of her arm and was totally healed.

We have seen God move in many miraculous ways. We have seen a woman healed from twelve tumors on her pancreas; she'd only had three months to live, but God. We've seen many babies born from barren wounds. A man, blind since birth, received his healing after the glory of God hit him at one of our services. Ear drums of the deaf have regenerated at our meetings. The crippled walked, and various diseases have been healed. One lady was having a seizure in the meeting and God healed her, and to top it off, she had a tumor the size of a boil egg on her leg and it disappeared. We have had people receive 100k, 84k, and 50k in our meetings as I release money miracles in the atmosphere. There was this one lady who came to our meeting to discredit who I was in the Lord. She said; she was there to prove I was a false prophet. I begin to release money miracles in the service, and told everyone to check their purses and wallets. So, she check her purse and nothing was in there. Then, before the service was over, I told everyone to check their purses and wallets again. The lady begin to check and found several hundred bills in the shape of a airplane in her purse. She told her testimony and have been following the ministry ever since. If God uses us, he can use anyone. All you have to do is T.A.P.

How to Become a Chaser

To become a glory chaser, there are several laws or principles you must apply.

1. "A chaser must learn and study what he or she is chasing".

Intense study of a subject will activate what we like to call the *law of attraction*. In this law, you will discover principles that inevitably lead you to your desired objective. As you, the chaser, sow seeds of interest, you will reap the attention of your target and set off a chain reaction that will draw them or it to you.

Here is a Scripture reference: *"Draw nigh to God, and he will draw nigh to you"* (James 4:8).

Drawing is a gravitational pull or magnet that forces two counter-parts to connect. I tell people all the time, every great man and woman of God I've had the privilege of coming in contact with, had no choice but to encounter me. You may say, "How is that?" Well, my curiosity and being an inquisitive student influenced their judgments about me, causing them to lower their guards and accept me into their inner circle.

You may say, "I don't want to chase after a man. I want to chase after God." Well, the same principle applies. If you're operating under the law of the student, it will cause the teacher to teach you. There is an old saying: when the student is ready, the teacher will come. Remember, the chase is always for learning purposes, whether it's directly from God or from an anointed mentor. So get prepared, because the teacher is coming.

2. Become a diligent seeker.

The Scriptures say, in Hebrews 11:6: *"But without faith it is impossible to please him: for he that cometh to God must believe that he is, and that **he is a rewarder of them that diligently seek him**"* (emphasis added). There is a reward system for diligence; once it's implemented the possibilities are endless. The word *diligent* is from the Greek word *spoudaios*, which means "prompt," "energetic," and "earnest." We must move promptly in the things of the spirit. Many believers need a thousand revelations and a million confirmations before they do the application. That's why they don't see the manifestations they desire.

It grieves me when I hear believers say, "That's the third or fourth confirmation." God has told them to start a business or write a book, but because they are waiting on another confirmation, they end up forfeiting the promise that was attached to the original blessing. Now, when that person finally starts pursuing their vision, they encounter strong resistance because the anointing is no longer on that particular word of promise. The enemy has had time to discover the plan, and the protection that was on that rhema word has been lifted. Now only binding and loosening will get it back. Quick obedience is the key.

Jesus said in Matthew 12:29: "*Or else how can one enter into a strong man's house, and spoil his goods, except he first bind the strong man? And then he will spoil his house.*" A lack of diligence will force you into the role of police officer. You must now storm the strong man's (the devil's) house, arrest (bind) him, and proceed to repossess the goods and promises he has stolen from you. Remember, the strong man is a thief; he does not possess goods, and what he has is stolen from you. If you fail to be diligent when God gives you a blessing for seeking Him, the enemy will gain the access codes to all of your blessings, and steal them right from under you without being detected.

The seeker must do more than seek to receive their reward. They must also be diligent. To be diligent, you must be energetic. That means you must be quick, prompt, and full of zeal. A person with zeal, but no revelation, will get further than someone with revelation and no zeal. The person with revelation thinks he has mastered that realm, because of his or her obtained knowledge on the subject. That person becomes comfortable because he or she believes their revelation will seal his or her position in that realm. In all actuality, too much revelation inhibits your ability to complete a project. That's why God wants us to go back to our first love (see Revelation 2:4) and regain the simplicity of a relationship with Him.

The body of Christ has turned obtaining God into a complex process. In reality, it only requires simple faith to receive Him. Now, the person with zeal will achieve quicker results because of his or her persistence, which means "to continue firmly despite obstacles." The person with zeal will face more warfare because of a lack of knowledge. But experience becomes their best teacher. Consistent victories increase their confidence and compel them to keep going from glory to glory. When we become diligent seekers of God, no devil in hell can block our blessings.

3. Endurance.

Last, but not least in the law or principle of becoming a glory chaser is endurance. Let me explain. In the course of your journey, you will encounter obstacles and hardships. In 2 Timothy 2:3, it says: "*Thou therefore endure hardship as a good solider of Jesus Christ.*" Our endurance of hardship will determine whether we are good soldiers for the Lord or not. The modern-day believer wants the white picket fence, the big house, and no trials and troubles. People of God, this is a false hope. Once you become a born-again believer the fight is on. Most believers want to be civilians and not soldiers. The definition of a civilian, according to Webster's dictionary, is "a person not serving in the military, as a firefighter, or as a policeman." When you're a civilian and not a solider for Christ, you can't fight the fiery darts of the enemy. When you're a civilian and not a solider, you can't bind or arrest the devil, because you don't carry the authority of a police officer. When you're a civilian, and you're not a solider in God's army, you are basically left defenseless.

Endurance will build up your authority just like boot camp builds up the muscles of a soldier. The objective of boot camp or hardship is to break down the weak elements inside an individual, so he or she may be reconfigured into a well-disciplined, combat-equipped, demon-killing machine. I don't know about you, but I refuse to have my destiny stolen from me. I am not afraid of facing my trials and hardships. I've heard stories of anointed men and women of God who didn't want to cast out demons because they retaliated. Jesus said in Mark 16:17, "*And **these signs shall follow them** that believe; In my name **shall they cast out devils**"* (emphasis added). This is a command, not a choice or suggestion. If we don't manifest these signs, then we were not assigned.

I have heard many say out of their own mouths, "if we don't mess with them, they won't mess with us." Let's just focus on the angels and God's glory." This is a cowardly statement made by passive believers who couldn't endure the warfare. So, when someone in a meeting is oppressed by a demon, a minister with that philosophy will pass them by, and try to avoid causing a disturbance. They leave it up to the atmosphere of glory to do the work for them. Then if that atmosphere is not strong enough, then that person will still be in bondage when they leave the meeting. When this happens, we must shift our attention to the anointing. The glory shows how powerful God is, but the anointing exposes how powerful man is.

The anointing reveals your true relationship with God. The measure of power that flows through you reveals how much you've been seeking God. Endurance is a form of works, just like the anointing. In the glory there is less work and warfare. However, I have seen many people become so lazy and dependent on the glory that, when it lifts, they cannot bring any form of deliverance to the captives. When we constantly depend on one facet of God, we start to lose ground in other realms of the spirit. In the glory, the Father fights for us. In the anointing, he allows us to stand up and fight for ourselves. This builds up our work ethic and endurance as soldiers in the Kingdom. With the anointing, we are more than civilians. Always remember, "*he that **endures to the end** shall be* *saved*" (Matthew 10:22). Therefore, let's keep a military mindset and remind ourselves daily that we are not only sons and daughters of God, but we are also soldiers in His army.

—m—

I pray that everyone who reads this chapter and these prayers becomes a glory chaser. Let their zeal line up with your will, Father God. Bless their feet as they chase the cloud of your glory. May the King of glory come in and live with them in their homes, jobs, relationships, bodies, and families, in Jesus name. Amen. T.A.P.

Chapter 2
Levels of Worship

What Are Levels of Worship?

There are different levels of worship that we can experience in the realms of God's presence. Each level will give us a different outlook and understanding of the principles of worship.

A level is a position from which other heights and depths are measured, and there are measurements in the spirit world that determine access into the unseen realms.

To access the spirit of faith, for instance, Jude 1:20 tells us: "*Building up yourselves on your most holy faith, praying in the Holy Ghost.*" To **build** means "to fashion or create; to develop or add to." The body of Christ uses the term "***Kingdom building.***" We must first build up that place where the King is. So, I ask the question, "Where is the King?" Well, according to Luke 17:21: "*Neither shall they say, Lo here! or, lo there! for, **behold, the kingdom of God is within you**"* (emphasis added). We must consider the truth that the Kingdom of God is within us. If we are torn to pieces on the inside, God's Kingdom is torn up as well. Therefore, we must rebuild the temple of God (1 Corinthians 6:19) and figure out the depth, width, and height of how to reconstruct His Kingdom. How do we do that? The answer is through worship. Let me explain why.

Where to Worship

We build God's Kingdom through worship. We also understand from (Luke 17:21) *that the Kingdom of God is within us.* If we are broken, so is the Kingdom of God. So, how do we rebuild the Kingdom within?

John 4:20=21 tells us, "*Our fathers worshipped in this mountain, and ye say, that in Jerusalem is the place where men ought to worship. Jesus saith unto her, Women, believe me, the hour cometh, when ye shall neither in this mountain, nor yet at Jerusalem, worship the Father.*" We see in this Scripture that the worship of God is not limited to a structure or geographical location. Oftentimes, pastors and leaders across the world believe their building or church is the dwelling place of the Holy Spirit. But the truth is that, He dwells in the vessels that worship Him "*in spirit and in truth*" (John 4:23). It's the individual Kingdom structure within us that determines the level of worship to which God will manifest.

Many people worship out of emotionalism and not in spirit and truth.

Anybody can praise, but only a true worshiper can worship God. According to the latter part of John 4:23, "***The Father seeketh such to worship him.***" (emphasis added). In worship, you may seek God, but it is not true worship until God the Father starts to seek you. When you seek the Father, it ignites a spiritual chain reaction that He can't resist the courting of. It's like an energy identical to His own love. Now, it's no longer you seeking the Father, but He is also seeking you.

Think about how important it is to be in a two-sided relationship. A sign that you have reached the vital point in the climax of worship is when your physical being experiences a numbing sensation. During this process, the atmosphere will grow silent, and you will tune out the sounds of earthly activities. Your awareness of chronological time will diminish as you embark on the journey to a "*kairos*" moment with God. The more in-depth and intense the worship is, the more the Lord involves Himself in your personal circumstances. **When you get into God's personal affairs through worship, then He gets into your personal affairs through blessings.**

Different Facets

In this section of the chapter, we will discuss the different facets of worship. Facets are different aspects or views of a person or subject; and our particular subject is worship. The word *worship* means "reverence for a sacred object" or "high esteem or devotion for a person." According to the biblical and spiritual view, *worship* means to "bow down, prostrate, or do obeisance to." It can also mean "to honor," "reverence," or "to pay homage to superior beings or powers such as men, angels, or God." It's most often used as an honor system paid to a deity, whether it is God or satan (the devil). It can also be either a private or public acknowledgement of that divine presence.

In the Bible, the Israelite patriarchs demonstrated the various stages of worship when they gave reverence to God and sacrificed to Him. They advanced from altars of the Tabernacle, and finally they built the Temple. The altars were built of stone and used by both individuals and groups in simple acts of worship and reverence. In both the Tabernacle and the Temple, worship was organized with a complex system of rituals and sacrifices that God outlined for Moses on Mount Sinai. The Temple was built during the reign of King Solomon. The Tabernacle was a portable sanctuary, or tent, that served as a place of worship for the Israelites while they wandered in the wilderness. Both the Tabernacle and the Temple typified God's dwelling with His people.

The Tabernacle, crafted specifically from God's instructions to Moses, stood in a court 150 feet long and seventy-five feet wide. The sides were covered with linen curtains fastened to sixty pillars of bronze. In the court were the altar of burnt offerings and the bronze laver that was used by the priests for ritual absolutions. The forty-five by fifteen foot wooden Tabernacle stood at the west end of the court. Inside was a veil that divided it into two parts, the holy place and the holy of holies. The Lord explained to me one day why He showed up so powerfully in the early 1900's and the 40's and 50's revivals. These meetings were so great because they were held in tents. The Lord said, "*I have always dwelt in tents.*" Now He dwells in the tents of men's heart. He showed me how the linens of the Tabernacle resembled "king" size bed sheets, typifying the private and intimate time He spends with His bride through worship.

The Lord told me that without this intimacy with the bridegroom, we cannot produce a breakthrough or a move of God, and we cannot birth out powerful ministries without this encounter. He explained to me how many people love the "wedding" of getting born again, but don't spend time in worship to get sanctified for the "honeymoon." The wedding is a one-time occasion, but the honeymoon is supposed to be an ongoing event. That is why the familiar passage in, Ephesians 5:25-27, reads: "*Husbands, love your wives even as Christ also loved the church, and gave himself for it; that he might **sanctify**, and **cleanse it** with the washing of the water by the word, that he might present it to himself a **glorious church**, **not having** a **spot** or **wrinkle**, or anything; but that it should be **holy** and **without blemish**"* (emphasis added).

I said to myself when I read this scripture, "The Lord is coming back for a supermodel wife!"

Then the Holy Spirit told me, "*If Jesus wants this type of wife, so should you.*"

So I asked the Lord, "How can I become that kind of bride for you?"

He responded, "*By becoming a worshiper.*"

Hebrews 10:2 reads: "*For then would they [sacrifices] not have ceased to be offered? Because that the **worshippers once purged** should have had **no more conscience of sins**"* (emphasis added). Wow! There is purging through worship and removal of being sin conscience. Through becoming a true worshiper, I can develop the characteristics and image of the bride described in Ephesians 5:25-27. So let's get on our knees and T.A.P.!

Different Approaches

The word approach means "to come near to or draw closer." In the next few sentences, I will define and give you revelation on different approaches to worship. Matthew 4:9–10 reads: "*And saith unto him, All these things will I give thee, if thou will **fall down** and **worship** me. Then saith Jesus unto him, Get thee hence, satan; for it is written, **Thou shall worship the Lord thy God**, and him only **shall thou serve**"* (emphasis added). "Worship" in this passage is translated from the Greek word ***proskuneo***, which means "to prostrate in homage." Its meaning is similar to the Hebrew word ***shachah***, translated as "worship" in most of the Old Testament instances; it means "to prostrate in homage," "to bend or crouch or stoop," or "to humble oneself."

Shachah is a physical act in worship that shows respect. For instance, the youth in some foreign countries honor an elder or someone in authority with physical reverence by bowing down and prostrating themselves in homage to that leader. During biblical and medieval times, this physical reverence was often required when approaching a king or some sort of royalty. A biblical example is given in Daniel 3:10–11:

> *"Thou, O king, hast made a decree, that every man that shall hear the sound of the cornet, flute, harp, sackbut, psaltery, and dulcimer, and all kinds of musick, shall **fall down** and **worship** the golden image: And whoso **falleth not down** and **worshippeth**, that he should cast into midst of a burning fiery furnace." [Emphasis added]*

In this instance "worship" is translated from the Hebrew word *seged*, which also means "prostrating oneself."

Nebuchadnezzar was not a godly king, but he knew the vital importance of the shachah approach of worship; he used it to determine whether someone lived or died. Shadrach, Meshach, and Abednego refused to worship this king. This act of defiance landed them in a fiery furnace. I wonder if our lack of shachah (worship) could land us in the fiery furnace of hell. It is this approach to worship that the devil wanted Jesus to partake of in (Matthew 4:9). The devil knows that through this form of worship, you surrender your rights and powers to whatever deity you're paying homage to; it is a statement that says you pledge allegiance, which means "loyalty to a nation, cause, or sovereign entity." During the medieval days, once a king, prince, or knight was sworn in, he would make his subjects bow down and swear an oath of loyalty. Satan knew if he could get Jesus to bow down and worship him, he would gain access to a partial control over heaven. Nebuchadnezzar knew the same thing when it came to the three Hebrew boys. The principle to learn here is if we, as the body of Christ, spent more time on our knees in shachah towards the Lord, we would see more power in our services.

Singing

The second form of worship is exemplified in Psalm 100:2, which tells us to "*serve the Lord with gladness;* **come before his presence with singing**" (emphasis added). This scripture tells us directly about how to come before the Lord, with worship through singing. Let's go back to Daniel 3:10, where the king made a decree that anyone who heard "*the* **sound** *of the cornet, flute, harp, sackbut, psaltery, and dulcimers, and* **all kinds of music**" *would* **fall down** *and* **worship** *his golden image.* Notice the prophetic pattern of music first, then the physical homage of worship.

Worship through this approach is the key ingredient to summon the glory of God down. It's the Greek word *latreuo*, which means "to minister to God" or "to do a service of a worshipper." Kings love to be entertained, especially through music. It was the spirit-filled sounds of David's harp that drove the evil spirit away from King Saul (1 Samuel 16:23). Much of the book of Psalms is composed of prophetic songs given to David by the Holy Spirit. These songs of David prophesied Jesus death and resurrection. Psalm 22:16-18 says:

> "*For dogs have compassed me: the assembly of the wicked have enclosed me: then* **pierced my hands** *and* **my feet.** *I may tell all my bones: they look and stare upon me. They* **part** *my* **garments** *among them, and* **cast lots** *upon my vesture.*" [Emphasis added].

This is a description of the crucifixion of Jesus Christ. King David was not crucified, so he wasn't referring to himself. The only person who fits these specific details was Jesus Christ.

Another of King David's prophetic songs was fulfilled by Jesus as He was dying on the cross at Calvary, as recorded in Matthew

27:46: "*And about the ninth hour Jesus cried with a loud voice, saying Eli, Eli, lama sabachthani? that is to say,* **My god, my god, why hast thou forsaken me?**" (Emphasis added.). The latter part is an exact quote from one of David's songs, Psalm 22:1: "**My god, my god, why hast thou forsaken me?**" (Emphasis added.). This song was written more than several generations prior to Jesus appearance on earth in human form.

There is power in songs. Music and singing are the main tools for ushering in God's presence. Hebrews 2:12 tells us, "*I will declare thy name unto my brethren, in the midst of the church* **will I sing praise unto thee.**" (emphasis added). Every church needs to be a church of praise and singing to the Lord, because *the Lord inhabits the praises of His people* (Psalm 22:3). We must make praise our habit, not our hobby. When we praise and then worship, we are ministering to God as a congregation. Often, people don't understand that the Lord loves to be ministered to. When we sing to the Lord in worship, its draws angelic activity. The devil (Lucifer) knew this principle and used it to lure the fallen angels in heaven. We must follow this principle of worship to activate angelic activity in our lives as well.

Judgment in Worship

Ministering to God is a form of worship that comes from the Greek word **latreuo**. Well, what does minister mean? The Hebrew word, **diyn**, is translated as "minister" in Psalm 9:8: "*He shall minister judgment to the people in uprightness.*" This word means "to judge or strive or contend for." So, according to the origin of this word, we are to judge people, places, or things. This is emphasized in 1 Corinthians 6:2–3: "*Do ye not know that* **the saints shall judge the world**? *And if the* **world shall be judged by you,** *are ye* **unworthy to judge** *the smallest matters? Know ye not that* **we shall judge the angels**? *How* *much more things that pertain to this life?"* (Emphasis added.) So we as ministers should understand that we are worthy to judge the world and the angels.

Saints, we need judgment back in the church, as long as our judgment is righteous, we can enforce that rule upon the earth. If you commit a crime and go before a judge in a court of law and tell him, "Your Honor, you can't judge me," I believe that your freedom will be taken away within that minute, and you will find yourself in prison. Like I said before, whatever is in the natural arena also applies to the spiritual arena. Even in biblical times we had judges, that's why we had the book of Judges. These people weren't perfect. However, just like a court appointed judge of natural law, these people were appointed by God to govern over spiritual laws. Judging or judgment is another way to worship the Lord. I know this is hard to swallow but a lack of judgment waters down your worship. Remember, in worship we judge our ourselves and our conduct before we come before the Lord's presence. When we do enter into His presence, conviction takes place, because of the areas we forgot to judge.

Conviction is judgment through God's grace. When someone gets sentenced to prison he has been **convicted** of a crime, conviction is good judgment. Grace is the probation period before the final judgment. We are saved by grace through faith, right? But what are we saved from? You guess it: "judgment". That's why we come boldly to the throne, through worship, asking for grace in a time of need. God is the lover of our soul, but He is also the judge of it. We must remember that, every time we approach the judge, we are being judged, not condemned. Worship the Lord in spirit and truth, and you will have the freedom from the prison of sin and lack. That's why we must let the oppressed go free and loose the bonds of wickedness through worship, fasting, and praying (see Isaiah 58:6).

Serving

The third form of worship is serving or ministering. The Hebrew word for "minister" is **sharath**. It means "to serve or wait on. The Greek word, **diakoneo**, is also translated as "minister," and literally means "to attend as a servant, to aid or service." Along a similar line, the Greek word **latreuo** exemplifies a form of worship by paying homage (worshipping) to God through serving Him. Mark 10:45 says, "For even the Son of man came not **to be ministered unto**, but to **minister**, and to give his life a ransom for many" (emphasis added). We must follow Jesus example of ministry and come before the Lord with the intention to minister to Him and wait on Him.

Philippians 3:3 says, "*For we are the circumcision, which worship God in the spirit, and rejoice in Christ Jesus, and have no confidence in the flesh.*" This interpretation of worship, or ministering to God, displays the purest form of servant hood to the Lord. The Scripture says, "*Let the Lord be magnified, which hath pleasure in the prosperity of his servant*" (Psalm 35: 27). God takes pleasure in prospering His servants, but if you're not serving how can He take pleasure in your prosperity?

Many people have no problem serving the Lord. However, they have an issue with serving man. The Scripture says in Galatians 5:13–14: "*For, brethren, ye have been called unto liberty; only use not liberty for an occasion to the flesh, but* **by love serve one another**. *For all the law is fulfilled in one word, even in this;* **thou shalt love (serve) thy neighbor as thyself**" (emphasis added). We must serve one another just as much as we serve God, because it's the Lord who commands us to do so. Worshipping God through the principles of serving will take you into spiritual abundance like no other form of worship. Serving your neighbor will access earthly abundance like no other form of worship principle. It triggers heavenly and earthly blessings to the worshipper. Both are precious in God's sight.

Worship His Brilliance

We must also worship God's brilliance, as typified by the Greek word *dox*, which means "praise," "worship," "glory," or "splendor." As I said in previous paragraphs, when we sing to the Lord in worship, it draws angelic activity. Lucifer knew this anointed principle, and he used it to lure the fallen angels in heaven. Satan enticed them to worship him in his glory and brilliance. In Ezekiel 28:17 *the Lord said that satan's **"heart was lifted up because of thy beauty** thou hast **corrupted their wisdom by reason of thy brightness** I will cast thee to the ground, I will lay thee before kings, that they may behold thee."* (emphasis added). See, when we worship in this fashion, by adorning the brightness of a deity, we either influence or corrupt our wisdom. The Hebrew word used for brightness here is *yiphah*, also meaning "splendor." Lucifer's heart was lifted up with pride through this type of worship, but also the angels that worshipped him, wisdom became corrupted.

Father God loves this type of worship, it focuses on His splendor, brilliance, brightness and radiance. God is a God of light and beauty. What stems from the worship of the Lord's brightness? The answer is clarified through the word "brightness" in 2 Thessalonians, translated from the Greek word *epiphaneia*, which means "manifestation" or "glorious display." When we worship according to God's brilliance and brightness, manifestations of His glory take place. If manifestations are not taking place in our meetings, it is because we are not singing or worshiping the Lord with songs that pay reverence to His brightness and brilliance.

In Malachi 4:2 we read: "*But unto you that fear [reverence unto worship] my name shall the **Sun of righteousness arise** with healing in His wings*" (emphasis added). Notice this Scripture depicts Jesus as the Sun, not the *son*, of righteousness. The Hebrew word translated as "sun" is *shemesh*, meaning "to be brilliant." This scripture acknowledges and pays reverence to the importance of the Lord's brightness. Also note that healing took place when the Sun of righteousness arose. How did He arise? Through worship! Healing, creative miracles, and deliverance come forth during worship. Knowing the different types of worship and how to access them is the key to successful crusades, church services, or meetings. T.A.P.

—m—

I pray right now, in the name of Jesus, the Sun of righteousness, that everyone who reads these approaches to worship shall receive healing in their bodies in Jesus Christ's holy name. May they become sanctified worshippers and grow in intimacy with the bridegroom (Jesus) in a more intense way. Let the sweet smelling aroma of worship come from each person's lips as he or she reads this. In Jesus name we pray!

Chapter 3
The Israel Principle

What Is Israel?

The word Israel is a transliteration of the Hebrew word *Yisrael*, representing the phrase "he will rule as God" or "the prince who prevails with God." This name was given to Jacob after he wrestled with the angel in Genesis 32:28: "*And he said, Thy name shall be called no more Jacob, but Israel: for as a prince hast thou power with God and with men, and hast prevailed.*" It became the collective national name of Jacob's twelve sons, or the twelve tribes. It was later used in a narrower sense as the title of the northern kingdom, differentiating it from Judah, the southern kingdom. After the Babylonian captivity, the returning exiles designated Israel as the name of their nation. Israel is the apple of God's eye; it would be foolish not to focus on what God's eye is on.

Israel is a nation in Palestine that the grandson of Abraham, Jacob, revisited in 1909 BC. It was enslaved later on by the Egyptian Empire. This anti-Semitic policy led the children of Israel into a four-hundred year oppression. In the spring of 1446 BC, the children of promise received their exodus from Egypt. By the summer of 1446 BC, the children of Israel reached Mount Sinai, and a covenant was given to Moses, which was called the Torah, or Mosaic law. In this law, God established the rules and guidelines that the people of that nation had to follow to obtain and keep the promise. The law created for the children of Israel was just a shadow of what was to come when the Messiah arrived to fulfill the whole covenant. Israel is not just a land, but a covenant promise between God and His people. Let's discover this land and its promises.

Magnify My Ministry

I was seeing wonderful and glorious healings and miracles, but I wanted more. I watched the *"It's Supernatural",* television show archives on the internet and found a particular guest I liked to watch over and over again. His name was David Herzog. He wasn't like most ministers I had encountered. He was young, he had style, he looked like a surfer, and most importantly, he was someone I could relate to, someone down to earth. So, I bought some books and materials he had published. He covered several topics I had already received revelation on regarding the glory, except for one. This one was about magnifying your ministry by supporting Israel. To magnify means "to increase in size; to seem more important or greater; to glorify or praise someone or something." Herzog made this claim, and I was forced to search out the principles in his statement.

I had already had a revelation about learning the Jewish heritage, but I had not known the significance of the geographical location of Israel. I was under the impression that Israel had broken covenant, and the church was the new Israel, set up to take its place. I had no idea I was operating under the spirit of replacement theology. After listening to David Herzog, I repented and started a journey to help these native ancestors.

Follow the Jew

To learn more about the Jewish heritage, I had to follow a Jew. Even though I had Jewish in my bloodline, I still wasn't a full-blooded Jew. So, Herzog was the perfect one. Most Jews probably would have stoned me for following them around, but David was cool.

My wife, Tora, and I traveled around the United States to attend his meetings. One day we were in Dallas at one of his meetings, and all of a sudden David said, "These guys follow me everywhere. "They are coming with me to Israel."

I looked at my wife and said, "I wonder who's going to pay for that ticket." But I nodded my head in agreement and said, "Yes, I am coming!" **I knew whatever I attached myself to would eventually connect itself to me**.

The following principle will allow you to operate in the double-portion principle that was given to Elisha. That principle says, "*As the Lord God liveth, and my soul liveth, I will never leave thee*" (see 2 Kings 2:1–11). I knew that, in following David, I would T.A.P. into a realm of the spirit that would benefit my ministry. The principle is called "Follow the Leader."

Rosh Hashanah 2012

David Herzog was having a "New Beginnings Festival" along with Robert Sterns, Sid Roth, and Paul Wilbur. I promised him at a meeting in San Antonio that I would go and support him. So I flew to Sedona, Arizona. The weather was different: hot in the daytime and cold at night. On one of the nights, Robert Sterns called me up out of the crowd and prophesied over me. He said, "You keep asking, 'When am I going to be next?' But God held you for such a time as this. And in six months, get ready!"

I had been celebrating the Jewish holidays with several Jewish friends and supporters of Israel, so I felt like this was the key ingredient to T.A.P. into the next level of the glory.

On the last night of the conference, David said to everyone, "This is one of my friends, all the way from Texas, and he is coming with us to Israel."

Again I nodded my head, and with a big smile on my face, I said to myself, "Yes, I am!"

Journey to the Holy Land

A couple of months before the Israel trip, I told the people in my ministry that, if God wanted me to go, He'd have to provide and show me signs and wonders in the heavens and on the earth. It was Saturday, August 3, during one of our Sabbath Day meetings that the Lord gave me a prophetic word. He said, "There will be a natural disaster that will hit the United States at the end of October. In the months following, revival will come to your ministry."

Our trip to Israel was scheduled around that time. Sure enough, Hurricane Sandy hit the East Coast on October 29, 2012. It was considered a perfect storm. It hit Newark, New Jersey, near the airport we had to fly out of on our trip to Tel Aviv in November. I was so busy preparing for other ministry work that I had given up on the idea of going to Israel. My staff then reminded me of the prophecy I had spoken in August about the natural disaster hitting the United States at the end of October.

Several days afterward, someone gave me the rest of the money for the Israel trip. God definitely gave me a sign and made me wonder. Then my wife gave me a prophetic Scripture: "*And that **repentance** and **remission of sin should be preached** in His name among all nations, beginning at Jerusalem*" (Luke 24:47 emphasis added). It was exactly what the trip was all about: repentance and remission of sins being preached in Israel and the other nations. I've noticed that many people in the church don't preach on the issue of sin. Their messages are full of what I like to call "greasy grace, laughter, tickles, and heavenly fairytales." I'm not referring to real holy laughter and the joy of the Lord, or true encounters from the throne room of heaven. I'm referring to the peachy-keen messages that gloss over the reality that we are in real demonic warfare. We preach grace to the church, and repentance to the sinner, and that's backward. We're supposed to preach grace to the sinners, so they know Jesus can save them in spite of their wrong doing, but we must preach repentance to the church because we know better. This was the great commission of Jesus Christ before His ascension. He said to preach repentance and remission of sins; first to the Jews (the church) and then to the Gentiles (the sinners/unbelievers).

Divine Connections

A couple of weeks before my Israel trip, I told a friend that I wanted to meet Kevin Basconi, a former guest on "*It's Supernatural!*", with Sid Roth. I thoroughly enjoyed Kevin's interview and wanted to purchase some of his materials. We talked about Kevin for about a week, and then I forgot about it.

Then, it was time to go to Israel. I flew into Newark, New Jersey, to meet with everyone for our connecting flight to Tel Aviv. To my surprise, Kevin Basconi and his wife, Kathy were both in the group! I said, "Kevin!" He turned around, and we talked like we had known each other for years.

Then Kevin said, "I want you to come with us on our bus for the trip. I like you for some reason." He proceeded to give me his personal number and told me to call him anytime. Out of the blue, Kevin's wife started prophesying to me about my ministry and how unusual and unique it would be. I then called my wife Tora, so Kathy could tell her the prophecy. Tora told me that during my flight to the New Jersey airport, manna and angel feathers had formed in her hands. We'd had angel feathers before, but not manna. It confirmed what Kevin Basconi's wife, Kathy had prophesied. I knew then that this trip was God-led.

I Am Here, O' Israel

A Muslim makes a pilgrimage to Mecca at least once in his or her lifetime. I believe Christians should do the same with Israel. To magnify my ministry, I had to understand why going to Israel would help. Then the Scripture popped into my spirit: "*Pray for the peace of Jerusalem: they shall prosper that love thee*" (Psalm 122:6, emphasis added). I asked myself did I really love Israel, and if so was I praying out of a genuine heart or just sheer principle. I then repented for my motives and actions towards this holy place.

When our group arrived in Israel, it was during a time of war. A lot of other tour groups had canceled their trips, but not us. When the missile alarm went off, they told us to go into the Holocaust museum, which seemed quite ironic. For two days we prayed for a cease fire. I told Kevin Basconi there was going to be a cease fire the following day. And, sure enough, the very next day, channel two news in Israel reported that there was a cease fire. Kevin looked at me and said, "You called it."

When we landed in Israel, an awareness of holiness hit me, in spite of the friction and conflict that surrounded us. During the trip, I felt it in my spirit to pray more for Israel. My soul kept screaming, "I am here, O' Israel, I am here." There is a pulling to assist Israel once you visit. Israel is so strong that it feels like the safest of the war-torn foreign nations. It is the place where our Lord Jesus will set up His Kingdom. I want to be there when he does. How about you?

New Angels Assigned

I met some new friends while I was in Israel. These friends included James Durham and his wife, Gloria. They were very good friends with Kevin. James has a heavy prophetic and seer anointing. One day he looked at me and said, "During this trip, if no one else receives, you will." God has assigned five new angels to your ministry, and He will reveal them to you as the days go by."

The very next morning, I walked down to the cafeteria for breakfast and saw Kevin. I went and sat down at the table with him. All of a sudden I felt the heavy presence of God flow through my body like electrical currents, it was waves of glory.

Kevin Basconi prophesied: "Wow, I see several angels all around you. One is for miracles, signs, and wonders. One is for money multiplication. And one is for healing."

I was so struck that, I didn't hear the other angels he named.

Everyone who sat next to me was touched by the angels that surrounded me. Know this: Kevin was not around when James prophesied about the five angels that were assigned to me. But, just the very next day, bam! I got that incredible confirmation. God is so awesome!

Manifestation Unfolded

It was the fourth day of the trip. On the previous day, Kevin had named the angels that were assigned to my ministry. This day was different. God started giving me the revelation for this book. I also prayed for several people's healing, and they were healed. That night at dinner several people asked me to pray for them. A couple from Australia stood out the most. I prayed for the wife, and oil started dripping from her hand. Then, she started shaking, and I told her God was giving her the spirit of counsel. She started to get loud at that point.

Her friend said to me, "Do you know what you just said?"

I responded, "No, what did I say?"

She proceeded to tell me, "You mentioned the spirit of counsel. Did you know they are both actually counselors?"

"No, I did not," I responded.

Many people approached to get some of the oil that dripped from the lady's hand. This occurrence was another confirmation that I had just T.A.P.-ed into an anointed principle.

Angel of Rain

On the day that we were scheduled to go to the Upper Room, we stopped by the Pool of Bethesda. Pastor James told me that I had an angel of holiness at my side. Previously, my staff and I had prayed for the spirit of holiness to be in our midst. James had given another word of confirmation.

We went to the Upper Room, but because there were other tour groups there as well, we did not have a lot of time. We then decided to go to the roof of the building to finish the tour. All of a sudden the Holy Spirit told me, He was releasing an angel of rain. I immediately told David Herzog and the others.

David responded, "Cool, the angel of rain."

I asked the Lord, "What is an angel of rain?" The Lord told me it was an angel of harvest. Now note at this time Israel was in a season of drought and needed rain. They usually received a mere two inches of rain the entire season, so the chances of rain were a million to one.

The next day, we were on our way to evangelize to the lost sheep of Israel about their Messiah. We were about to get on the bus when it started to rain. The people on the tour bus looked at me as it poured and poured.

David came to me and said, "Well, you prayed for rain. Now, pray to make it stop so we can finish this tour!" He joked.

We had arrived at our destination, and were preparing to get off the bus when, the rain suddenly stopped. I led more people to Jesus than anyone on the tour. The people repented with tears in their eyes. When we returned to the bus it started to rain again. The Lord had stopped the rain so we could go win souls, and then He finished pouring out His Spirit. Remember, what happens in the natural is also happening in the spirit.

For, the next several days, it rained until it started to flood. Our tour guide, Mookie, said, "I don't know what you guys did, but if a group of Americans comes to Israel and it begins to rain, then we know they are from God. If not, then we know they are not, especially in this season because we don't see rain in this season."

God had confirmed His word to me once again with signs following. And, He told me about the other angel that was assigned to my ministry: the angel of rain. T.A.P!

What Did You Receive?

I finally arrived back in the states, and everyone was so excited to hear the stories of all that I had received. I was really tired from the trip, so I rested.

We had a meeting to attend in Austin, Texas, with Mahesh Chavda. When we arrived in Austin, several members of the church started to converse with us. I told them I had just returned from Israel and told them the different stories about the angels. Then the Holy Spirit told me to release the angel of rain in Austin. So I told the people I was releasing the angel of rain to them.

Just as soon as I said that, all those who were in that circle started to smell a citrus aroma. They became drunk in the spirit. Then a young lady who had been nowhere near the group, came up to us with a drawing of what was going to happen in the service that night. Everyone was shocked. It was a drawing of a hand with rain falling into it. The anointing grew stronger when she revealed that picture. I laid my hands on people's eyes and they started to see in the spirit and begin to prophesy.

Mahesh Prophecy

The man of God started teaching. Then, he stopped for a moment and began to prophesy. He turned around and looked right at me and started telling me about how I was going to write a book. He asked me the name of it.

I responded, T.A.P. "*The Anointed Principles*" of God.

Then Mahesh said, "Finish the book. I want a copy of it." He laid hands on my wife and me and said, "You have a powerful deliverance ministry. Go forward and do great exploits."

It was then time to pray for the sick. The man of God said, "Whoever is deaf in their ears, raise your hands." There was a deaf lady standing next to me with her translator. She raised her hand. Mahesh then said to the church, "If you have the healing gift, go lay hands on the deaf, and they will hear." So I turned to the lady and asked if I could pray for her; she insisted that I pray. I did, and her ears became hot, and then she heard a popping sound. And suddenly, she was able to hear. Praise God!

We left Austin excited about what had happened. But it wasn't over just yet.

I Did Receive

In the week after our trip to Austin, I was still not sure what all I had received, or if I had I received at all. We had already seen the eyes of the blind opened, the deaf gain their hearing, the lame walk, and the diseased cured. Oil dripped, and angel feathers appeared before my trip to Israel. But I wanted to see more of the supernatural. Sometimes, you get so familiar with the supernatural that it starts to seem natural to you, then the excitement begins to diminish. Then you lose your spiritual hunger for more of the impossible.

The following day, my wife, mother-in-law, and daughter were all in the car after leaving a store. Suddenly, my wife's foot slipped off the brake, and she sped into ongoing traffic. The cars were coming at seventy to eighty miles per hour, so she steered into the third lane. At that moment, a car barreled directly at them from the left side.

The next thing you are about to hear is a miracle from God. Two eyewitnesses saw this happen. My mother-in-law said that time seemed to stop and everything went in slow motion. My wife screamed, "Oh my God!" Instead of hitting them, the car came through the backseat on the driver's side, went through the car, and traveled through my daughter's body. My wife saw the other car inside of our car through the rearview mirror. It then went out through the opposite side of our car and kept going. There was no damage or broken glass, not even a scratch. This was the supernatural sign I had been looking for. This was the introduction to the second assigned angel, which was the angel of miracles, signs, and wonders.

Supernatural Travel

It was Christmas Eve, and there was a lot of traffic from last minute shoppers out on the roads. My wife and I drove to the Humble area from the southwest side of Houston, about an hour's drive from where we lived. We were picking up the children of a friend, so they could spend the night at our home. We left her home at 7:50 p.m.

As we drove, we played two worship songs of, about five minutes apiece. Fog covered over the windows, and my wife struggled to wipe it away. The children said they felt dizzy. I then looked out the window and saw that our surroundings were different. I saw the sign for the exit that would take us to our street. We called the children's mother and asked her how long it had been since we left her house. She said about fifteen minutes. We told her we were already on the other side of town, up the street from our home. The children said, "That's weird! We made it home in fifteen minutes when it normally takes an hour or more to get there.

We had actually been transported in the spirit. This had happened to us once before in Brazoria, Texas. I had a meeting to go to, but our GPS system said it would take an hour and forty-five minutes for us to get there. So, we began to worship. All of a sudden, a diamond dropped onto our dashboard. We were in traffic, on a section of road where there were no exits for miles. When the diamond fell, we looked around, and there were no cars in sight.

"Where did they go?" the children asked. We told them we didn't know. We then saw a sign that read, "Next stop: Brazoria, Texas." That was our exit. The GPS had said it would take us one hour and forty-five minutes. We were translated in the glory an hour and twenty-five minutes ahead of time. We had driven for only twenty-minutes.

Why am I telling you these stories? To show you the supernatural benefit of supporting and loving Israel. Pray for the peace of Jerusalem. God promises to bless those who bless Israel and curse those who curse them (Genesis 12:3). Let this be more than a principle you follow; make it a habit. And, remember when I mentioned releasing the angel of rain in Austin? The next day, it began to rain there. I really did receive, and I believe you can too. T.A.P.

—⁓—

Lord Jesus, may everyone within the sound of my voice receive a prophetic insight about supporting Israel and the Jewish people. Let us rise up and stand with them in these trying times. Let us not forget that we are grafted in and that we serve a Jewish King. May both Jew and Gentile receive the blessings of Abraham and the new covenant promises of the Jewish Messiah Jesus Christ. Shalom, shalom, shalom!

Chapter 4
Communion in the Spirit

The Power of Communion

In this chapter I will explain the importance of communion, or communication with the Holy Spirit. I will also elaborate on the Holy Spirit's vital role in the day-to-day activities of a Christian's walk with the Lord. During this process of evaluation of the Spirit, you will receive an impartation for more of the Holy Spirit's presence in your life. So, let's T.A.P. into the world of the Holy Spirit.

Let's' start off by defining what communion is. "Communion" is translated from the Greek word *koinonia*, which means "partnership or fellowship, social intercourse or intimacy," or "benefaction." A benefaction is a charitable donation or gift. Communion with the Spirit is not just sharing; it is also a gift, so, we must reciprocate the gift of communion or communication to show our appreciation for Him. Communion also means a "mutual sharing of feelings and thoughts." *Koinonia* also means "partnership" in the Greek. The word partnership means "two or more persons who run a business together and share in the profits and losses." Wow! So, that means we are business partners and co-C.E.O.s with the Holy Spirit as we oversee the daily operations of Father God's business. Mark 16:20 reads, "*And they went forth, and preached everywhere,*

56

*the Lord **working with them**, and confirming the word with signs follow-ing.*" (emphasis added) Amen! The Scripture tells us the Lord was working **with** them not *for* them.

The body of Christ has a slothful spirit. They expect the Lord to do Kingdom business *for* them. There is an excuse they love to use to explain this dilemma: "I am just waiting on the Lord." I hate to be a burden breaker, but the Lord is waiting on us to get to work. The body of Christ doesn't understand this concept because the traditions of men have taught us that we can't get God to move when we want Him to. I was taught growing up that you can't talk to God the wrong way because He might strike you down. But once I was filled with the Holy Spirit and began to dig into the Word, I realized that God allows people to express their feelings to Him and to negotiate with Him.

Here are some scriptural examples:

Genesis 18:17: "*And the LORD said, Shall I hide from Abraham that thing which I do?*"

In this passage, the Lord was on the verge of destroying Sodom and Gomorrah for their sins. But, before He made a decision on the earth, He consulted with His business partner, Abraham, who in response, started to negotiate with God. The following verse tells us about the end of the negotiations. Genesis 18:32-33: "*And he said, Oh let not the LORD be angry, and I will speak yet but this once: Peradventure ten shall be found there. And he said, I will not destroy it for ten's sake. And the LORD went His way, as soon as, he had left [**communing with Abraham**]; and Abraham returned unto his place*" (emphasis added). This emphasizes the power of communication, or communion. Abraham negotiated with God on Sodom and Gomorrah's behalf.

Matthew 15:26–28: *"But he answered and said, It is not meet to take the children's bread and to cast it to the dogs. And she said, Truth, Lord: yet the dogs eat of the crumbs, which fall from their master's table. Then Jesus answered and said unto her, O woman, great is thy faith: be it unto thee even as thou wilt. And her daughter was made whole from that very hour."* This Gentile woman was not even in the covenant or filled with the Holy Ghost. But her faith opened communication, so she negotiated with God, even though it wasn't in His will to reach out to her. In Matthew 15:24 He stated, *"I am not sent, but unto the lost sheep of the house of Israel."* Because this Gentile woman knew how to communicate with God through the faith principle, she was able to change the mind of God. T.A.P.!

The list goes on and on. Hezekiah prayed thirty words, and the Lord changed His mind and gave him fifteen more years of life. You can find that story in 2 Kings 20:1-6. What I am saying here people, is that, if we get the understanding that the Lord wants us to communicate with Him in the spirit truthfully, honestly and even emotionally, then we will see more manifestations of the Spirit in the earthly realm. So let's T.A.P.!

Who Is the Holy Spirit?

Before we embark on the journey of discovering the origins and attributes of the Holy Spirit, let me first define what He is not. I like the way Dr. Mike Murdock tells us about the Holy Spirit in "The 3 Most Important Things in Your Life," found at http://timkyara.wordpress.com/books-i-am-reading/the-3-most-important-things-in-your-life-mike-murdock/: "He is not water (tho' refreshes like one), wind (tho' he moves like one), fire (tho' he purifies like one) or white dove (tho' He is gentle like one); He is not an 'it' but rather a Him. He is a person, not just a presence."

Many view the Holy Spirit as an energy force from God that gets released into the atmosphere when we are in a church service. Some identify Him as the goose bumps or emotional reactions that people receive during a time of worship. I grew up with a traditional Baptist background. When someone would "catch" the Holy Ghost in a service, the ushers would begin to fan him or her. They would escort that person out of the building if he or she became too much of a distraction. People, me included, would turn around in their seats staring at this person like he or she had lost it. But even as a little boy, I questioned, "If that is the Holy Ghost, why would they escort God out of the building?" I asked myself, "If that's not the Holy Ghost and it's just emotionalism, what is the Holy Ghost, and how does He operate?"

I Need to Know Him

In the previous segment, I explained who the Holy Spirit is not. Now let me share what I have learned about who He is from my own knowledge, experiences and encounters with Him. The Holy Spirit is the third person of the triune Godhead. Matthew 28:19 and 2 Corinthians 13:14 speak of the three: Father, Son, and Holy Spirit. The word spirit in the Old Testament is almost always the translation of the Hebrew word *ruwach*, as in Zechariah 4:6: "*This is the word of the LORD unto Zerubbabel, saying, Not by might, nor by power, but by my spirit, saith the LORD of hosts*" (emphasis added). The word *ruwach* means "breath," "wind," "touch", or "to make a quick understanding of." In the New Testament, "spirit" is almost always translated from the Greek word *pneuma*, similar in meaning to *ruwach*.

I understand now why ministers blow their breath on the audience and say words like "touch," and the crowd feels a tangible reaction of the Spirit manifesting in an unearthly matter. It is possible that the Holy Spirit is using the minister as a host to make those gestures and statements, such as "touch," so He can introduce Himself to the people. We must understand that the Holy Spirit is not just the average spirit you may see in a horror movie or on a paranormal reality show. What makes the Holy Spirit stand out in a class of His own? It's that He is holy!

What is holy? "Holy" is translated from a form of the Hebrew word *qadash*; it means; "to make, pronounce, or observe as clean." It also means "consecrate, prepare, proclaim, purify, or sanctify oneself wholly." Similarly, in the New Testament, the Greek word *hieros* means "sacred and set apart for God." All definitions paint a beautiful picture of who and what the Holy Spirit means to us in our walk with God. The infilling and communion with the Holy Spirit is a vital part of our lives once we receive Jesus Christ as our savior. In fact, it is only through the drawing of the Father's Spirit, the Holy Spirit that we can come to Jesus. In John 6:44 Jesus said, *"No man can come to me, except the Father which hath sent me **draw him**; and I will **raise him up** at the last day."* (emphasis added). How will he draw and raise us up, through the Holy Spirit of course. Romans 8:11 says: *But if the **Spirit of him that raised up Jesus from the dead** dwell in you, he that raised up Christ from the dead shall also quicken your mortal bodies **by his Spirit that dwelleth in you**.* (emphasis added). It's the Holy Spirit that raises us from the dead. This is one of the many Scripture references that show the importance of the Holy Spirit before and after the born-again conversion. T.A.P.!

God, the Holy Spirit, and Jesus

We are three-part beings according to 1 Thessalonians 5:23: *"I pray God your whole **spirit** and **soul** and **body** be preserved blameless"* (emphasis added). We were made in God's image according to Genesis 1:26–27. The beginning of verse twenty-six says: *"And God* said, *Let **us** make man in **our** image, after **our** likeness.*" (emphasis added). Notice that God said "**our**" and "**us**" He referred to Himself in a plural sense. Those who were in attendance at this meeting were God the Father, God the Son, and God the Holy Spirit. But even though He was conversing with three, He was speaking to Himself.

Matthew 28:19 reads, *"Go ye therefore, and teach all nations, baptizing them **in the name** of the Father, and of the Son, and of the Holy Ghost"* (emphasis added). He said to baptize them in the "**name**," not "**names**." This word is singular not plural. The Lord is making the statement that He has one name but three personalities. Well, what name should we use then? God, Jesus, or the Holy Spirit?

Philippians 2:9–11 reads:

> *"Wherefore **God hath** highly exalted him [Jesus], and **given him a name** which is **above every name**. That at the **name of Jesus** every knee should bow, of thing in **heaven**, and things in **earth**, and things under the earth. And that every tongue should confess that **Jesus Christ is Lord,** to the glory of God the Father."* [Emphasis added]

Acts 2:38 tells us, *"Then Peter said unto them, Repent, and be baptized every one of you in the **name of Jesus Christ** for the remission of sins, and ye shall receive the gift of the Holy Ghost"* (emphasis added). Pay attention to what the apostle Peter did: he received the commission from Jesus to baptize in the name of the Father, Son, and Holy Spirit. Why did he baptize these people in Acts 2:38 only in the name of Jesus and not God or the Holy Spirit? Was Peter backsliding again and rebelling against God? No! He caught the revelation that Jesus Christ was all three of the Godhead in one. According to Colossians 2:9, *"In Him dwelleth all the **fullness** of the **Godhead** bodily"* (emphasis added). Jesus was God the Father, God the Son, and God the Spirit in one body.

In Romans 13:14 He is referred to as the "Lord Jesus Christ." "Lord" is a translation of the Greek *kurios*, meaning "master" or "father" "Jesus" is from the Greek *Iesous*, which means "Jehovah-saved"; and "Christ" is from the Greek word *Christos*, "the anointed one" or "the Messiah," which is a description of God's Spirit. Back in Acts 2:38 we read, "*And ye shall receive the gift of the Holy Ghost.*" So, if you get baptized in the name of Jesus Christ for remission of sins, you will receive the gift of the Holy Spirit. Why would you need the Holy Spirit if you already have the fullness of the Godhead when you receive Jesus? Because, you receive God in your heart when you receive Jesus; but, when you receive the infilling of the Holy Spirit by accepting God's gift, you receive power to operate the way Jesus did on the earth.

Jesus Needed Him

Modern day Christians know they cannot cast out demons or do great exploits for God, unless it's through the name of Jesus Christ, just as Christians in New Testament times knew. I would like to propose a question: what name did Jesus use to cast out demons and heal the sick? There is no indication in any of the gospels that he used a name when performing miracles. There is also no indication of a name that Old Testament prophets may have used. Since prophets had no knowledge of the name Jesus yet, and since Jesus did not use his own name, we must wonder, where did their source of power for performing miracles come from.

Look at Matthew 12:28, where Jesus makes this statement, "*But if I cast out devils by the **Spirit of God**, then the **kingdom of God is come** unto you.*" (emphasis added). Jesus performed miracles through the power of the Holy Spirit. He revealed the Spirit of God as His source of power. Unfortunately, in modern day society, we to ignore the sufficiency of the Holy Spirit. Jesus was saying, "I have my power and my ministry because of the Spirit of God, and when the Spirit of God moves, the whole Kingdom of God moves." Did you get that? When the Spirit of God moves the whole Kingdom of God moves!

The Holy Spirit is just as important as Jesus and God. I'll explain why I have this bold theory. Let's go deeper into the Scriptures to Matthew 12:31-32. Remember, in these verses Jesus is speaking of Himself; also remember that Jesus said in John 17:17, "***Thy word is truth.***" (emphasis added). In Matthew 12:31 Jesus says, "*Wherefore I [Jesus] say unto you, All manner of sin and blasphemy shall be forgiven unto men: but the **blasphemy against the Holy Ghost** shall not be forgiven unto men.*" "Blasphemy" in the New Testament is a transliteration of the Greek word ***blasphemia***, meaning "vilifying" or "speaking evil." Similarly, an Old Testament word translated as "blasphemy" is the Hebrew word ***neatsah***, meaning "scorn" or "contempt." This verse is saying that when you scorn, contempt, or speak evil of the Holy Spirit, you will not be forgiven. In 1 Thessalonians 5:19, we are told, "***Quench not the Spirit.***" Then, in Ephesians 4:30, we are exhorted, "*And **grieve not the Holy Spirit of God**, whereby ye are sealed unto the day of redemption.*" (emphasis added). These passages of scripture did not mention quenching or grieving God or Jesus. No, it says not to quench or grieve the Spirit.

Matthew 12:32 warns us, "*And **whosoever speaketh a word against the Son of man {Jesus}, it shall be forgiven him;** but whosoever **speaketh against the Holy Ghost**, it **shall not be forgiven him**, neither in this world, neither in the world to come.*" (emphasis added). Jesus was saying that we could speak freely against Him, but if we say something against the movement of God Spirit or deny His status as God, then we won't be forgiven.

Jesus was talking with His disciples in John 14: 9–11:

*"Jesus said unto him, Have I been so long time with you, and yet hast thou not known me, Philip? **He that hath seen me hath seen the Father;** and how sayest thou then, Show us the Father? Believest thou not that **I am in the Father, and the Father in me**? The words that I [Jesus] speak unto you I speak not of myself; but **the Father that dwell in me, he doeth the works.** Believe me that **I am in the Father, and the Father in me;** or else **believe me for the very work's sake.**" [Emphasis added]*

Wow! Jesus said the Father who dwells in Him does the work. Remember, in Matthew 12:28 Jesus admitted that He did the work (casting out devils) by the Spirit of God. But here, He says "*the Father in Me*" does the work. Who is the "*Father in Me*"? Yes, the Holy Spirit! So the Father (God) in Jesus is really the Holy Spirit. Notice in verse eleven of John 14 where Jesus says, "If you don't believe Me, at least believe in the works." What works? The works of the Spirit, of course. It's through the works, or manifestation, of the Holy Spirit that we receive or see miracles.

Who's Your Daddy?

Matthew 1:18 tells us: "*Now the birth of Jesus Christ was on this wise: When as his mother Mary was espoused to Joseph, before they came together, she was found with **child of the Holy Ghost**.*" (emphasis added). If you skip down to Matthew 1:20, it says, "*But while he [Joseph] thought on these things, behold, the angel of the LORD appeared unto him in a dream, saying, Joseph, thou son of David, fear not to take unto thee Mary thy wife: for that which is **conceived in her is of the Holy Ghost**.*"

Nine times out of ten, or ten times out of ten, if a statement or a quote is mentioned twice in the Bible, you take it to the bank. So am I saying Jesus is not the Son of God, but the Son of the Holy

Ghost? No! But I am saying He is the Son of both because *"God is a Spirit"* (John 4:24). What Spirit? The Holy Spirit! Jesus is God's body according to John 1:14: *"And the word was made flesh."* God the Father is the soul according to Hebrews 10:38; *"Now the just shall live by faith; But if any man draw back, **My soul** shall have no pleasure in him."* (emphasis added). See, the Father is the soul because He is the only one in the Godhead, who insists on His will being done.

The will comes from the soul realm, which is, the mind, the free will, and the emotions. Jesus always mentions the Father's will and how He only wanted to please the Father. God the Father's soul has emotions: *"God so loved the world"* (John 3:16). Love is an emotion. In fact *"God is love"* (1 John 4:8). To finalize the theory that God the Father is the soul of the Godhead, God the Father came up with the idea to make man (see Genesis 1:26). Ideas come from the mind, which is the soulish realm. The Holy Spirit is God's spirit according to John 4:24 and 2 Corinthians 3:17. You get three for the price of one. Get it? Jesus also referred to Himself as the "Son of man." That is biblical truth as well. Mark 14:62 reads*: "Jesus said, I am [God]: and ye shall see the **Son of man** sitting on the right hand of power, and coming on the clouds of heaven."* (emphasis added). Jesus is in heaven, at the right hand of God, as the Son of God and the Son of man. Jesus was just as much a man as He was God.

In 1 Corinthians 15:45, 47, we read: *"And so it is written, The **first man Adam** was made a living soul; the **last Adam** was made a quickening spirit."* This shows us again that Jesus, who is the last Adam, was made a spirit but still was compared to Adam, who was a man. Why does the Scripture call Jesus "the last Adam"? Maybe because Adam was considered to be the first Jesus on earth. The first Adam was born of a supernatural birth as well. He came neither from the womb of a woman or the seed of a man. He was born directly from mother earth and the breath (spirit) of Father God. But, he messed up the close relationship God intended between Him and mankind. Adam lost his position, and failed his mission.

The last Adam (Jesus) came to earth in the form of a man to redeem us and restore communion between the Heavenly Father and His children. That is what the Scripture says in Matthew 1:23: "*Behold, a virgin shall be with child, and shall bring forth a son, and they shall call His name Emmanuel, which being interpreted is, God with us.*" I did not write this section to confuse the reader or give the body of Christ some new doctrine. My main purpose is to emphasize the importance of the Holy Spirit.

Mark 1:10 tells us:

> "*And straightway coming up out of the water, he saw the heavens opened and **the Spirit** like a dove descending upon him: And there came a **voice from heaven**, saying, Thou art my beloved Son, in whom I am well pleased. And immediately **the spirit driveth Him** [Jesus] into the wilderness.*" [Emphasis added]

It wasn't until the Spirit descended like a dove that John heard the voice that claimed Jesus as His son. It was the voice of the Spirit. We as humans cannot handle the voice of God the Father, it must be filtered through the voice of the Holy Spirit. Let's T.A.P. into this voice.

Pray the Father

John 14:16 is very interesting. It reads, "*And **I will pray the Father**, and he shall give you another Comforter, that He may abide with you forever.*" (emphasis added). I love the first part of this verse. Jesus said, "***I will pray the Father.***" It seems like a misuse of grammar. Perhaps

66

it should read, "*I will pray to the Father.*" This verse is referring to a particular prayer Jesus was going to administer to His disciples. But why did He state it in that way? One day, I asked the Holy Spirit what Jesus was saying here. The Holy Spirit revealed to me that the statement "*I will pray the Father*" meant He would pray in the Holy Spirit. Praying in the Holy Spirit is praying directly to the Father (see 1 Corinthians 14:2).

Let me break it down. Jesus was aware of the gift of tongues because, in Mark 16:17, it reads, "*And these signs shall follow them that believe; In My name shall they cast out devils; they shall speak with new tongues*" (emphasis added). Before His ascension He was explaining to His disciples the detailed manifestation of a true believer. Remember, the disciples had already been operating in certain gifts such as casting out demons and healing the sick (Mark 10:1), but the manifestation of speaking in tongues had not been revealed to them yet. In Acts 2:38, Peter told the crowd to repent and be baptized and receive the Holy Spirit. Peter knew that Jesus had told them what a New Testament believer would look like (Mark 16:17). Also, we see it in Acts 19:2, where Paul asked certain disciples in Ephesus if they had received the Holy Ghost after believing. Paul was asking them if they had been baptized in the Holy Spirit, for baptism was the subject in (verse three). It was customary at that time for a New Testament believer to receive the baptism of the Holy Spirit. During this encounter, an experience took place. Acts 19:6 tells us, "*And when Paul had laid his hands upon them, the Holy Ghost came on them; and they spake with tongues, and prophesied*" (emphasis added).

Speaking in tongues was the prayer language Jesus spoke of in (Mark 16:17). But, note that Jesus would not want us to have something He did not know or have Himself. In 1 Peter 2:21, it says, "*For even hereunto were ye called: because Christ also suffered for us, leaving us an example, that ye should follow his steps.*" (emphasis added). This

Scripture tells us that He left us an example. In Mark 16, He left an explanation and an example of the sign that would differentiate between those that were His, and those that were not. But, is there an earthly example of Jesus using tongues in Scripture? Yes, there is! Go with me to John 11:33: "*When Jesus therefore saw her weeping, and the Jews also weeping which came with her, **he groaned in the spirit**, and was troubled*" (emphasis added). Wow! Jesus groaned in the spirit not in the flesh. Is there another New Testament Scripture that describes this groaning during the Spirit encounter?

Well, let's look at Romans 8:26: "*Likewise the Spirit also helpeth our infirmities: for **we know not what we should pray** for as we ought; but the **Spirit itself maketh intercession for us with groanings** which cannot be uttered*" (emphasis added). This verse indicates to me that groaning is connected to prayer, the Holy Spirit, and intercession. It even ties into Ephesians 6:18: "*Praying always with all prayer and supplication in the Spirit, and watching there unto with all perseverance and supplication for all saints.*" Our English word supplication here is translated from the Greek word **deesis**, meaning "petition, prayer, request, or supplication."

In the Old Testament, "supplication" is often translated from the Hebrew word **chanan**, which means "to entreat, to show favor, or to have mercy." So it would make sense that Jesus was making supplication as He groaned in the Spirit for Lazarus. He favored him and showed him mercy. It hurt Jesus when Lazarus died; the Bible tells us, "*Jesus wept*" (John 11:35). In John 11:33 Jesus groaned in the spirit, after that He wept in John 11:35. So, we can not associate groaning and weeping as the same thing. Remember, both where done at separate time frames of the scripture. After Jesus groaned in the Spirit, in the very next sentence He said, "*Where have you laid him?*" (John 11:34). Immediately after He groaned in the Spirit, He was ready to go raise the dead. Jude 1:20 speaks of this kind of action. It reads "*But ye, beloved, **building up yourselves in*** *your most Holy faith, **praying in the Holy Ghost**.*" It takes the gift of faith to raise the dead. This was the same gift of faith that the apostle of faith, Smith Wigglesworth, was known for in his ministry. He raised many people from the dead. Smith was a man who constantly prayed in the Spirit. Jesus gave us a principle to follow, so that we might do great miracles. Perhaps those in attendance didn't realize it, but if we can look past our theological mindsets, maybe just maybe, we can see how praying in the Holy Ghost was applied by Jesus at the tomb of Lazarus. So, as we "pray the Father," we should start seeing the dead begin to rise in our churches, streets, missions, and outreaches. T.A.P.!

—⁓—

I pray in the name of Jesus Christ that everyone who reads this chapter, and prays, gets baptized in the Holy Ghost and fire! Lord, according to Luke 11:13, "If ye then, being evil, know how to give good gifts unto your children: how much more shall your heavenly Father give the Holy Spirit to them that ask him? Receive the Holy Spirit, and begin to speak in tongues as the spirit gives utterances.

Chapter 5
My Conversion

The story of my conversion is all facts and no fiction. It starts with tragedy, but ends in triumph. It may seem raw and uncut, but it depicts the harsh reality of the strongholds the devil has on certain parts of society today. I will give you the PG-13 version of the story to protect certain people's identities and lives. Certain information I will not omit. These statements cannot be used to reopen cases that have been closed. That is double-jeopardy, according to the law. So, let's begin.

My name is Shawn Anthony Morris. I was born in New Orleans, Louisiana, on December 10, 1979, to Audrill Morris and Bill Hurst. From day one, my biological father denied that I was his. He and his mother, brothers, and sisters were well-known drug dealers and murderers in the city. My mother's side of the family was a little different, although they lived around the crime-infested Calliope Projects. My mother grew up in a fairly decent household with both mother and father in the home. There was one issue: my grandparents had six kids, but my mother was the only one who was dark-skinned. The rest of her siblings were light-skinned with blue or green eyes and looked Caucasian.

My mother's family was mixed with Jewish, French, Indian, and African heritages. My father's side was Native American, Irish, Italian, and African. Because of my mother's dark complexion, her siblings teased her and insisted that she was adopted. She was the literal black sheep of the family. So, my mother grew up bitter, and she was plagued by a spirit of rejection that opened her up to a manic-depressive spirit later in life.

My Birth

I was born prematurely. I had a hole in my heart, and the doctors thought I wasn't going to make it. But I did! The devil tries to kill many prophets at birth because he has a glimpse of their future and destiny. He tries his best to abort the blessing before it's fully developed. He tried to kill Moses at birth (Exodus 1:16), as well as our Messiah Jesus Christ (Matthew 2:16–18). When I was two years old, one of my mother's boyfriends tried to burn me with acid because my mother refused to be with him. Then, she met my step-father, Reginald Thompson, who was six feet, three inches tall and two hundred plus pounds. He ran the other guy off. Not long after that, my mother married Reginald. When I was born, my biological father denied me and neglected his responsibilities. My mother grew bitter towards him and eventually took it out on me. Because my biological father rejected me as his child, the spirit of rejection and depression took a toll on my mother. She began to abuse me physically by burning me with cigarettes or beating me with any object she could find. Every time she would look at me, she reminded me that I looked like my father. She would humiliate me in front of my siblings and relatives, and the insults would be considered jokes. I grew up as the black sheep of the family, just like she did, and that verbal abuse lasted throughout my childhood and adulthood.

Now the Saga Begins

Marrying Reginald gave my mother a brief respite of acceptance, a way to escape her childhood of rejection and the hardship of raising a child on her own. My deadbeat father denied a child (me) who looked just like him. They took him to court for child support once; the judge was going to lock him up for denying me, because I looked so much like him. I had no father figure or male role model to look up to, only the guys on the streets and my stepfather. But there was a little secret that my mother's husband was hiding. He was addicted to crack cocaine a drug that hit America at that time like an unstoppable plague. I had no chances growing up. I had a manic-depressive mother who popped pills from time to time to escape reality. I had a crack dealer for a father, who was now in prison, and a crack addict for a stepfather. So, the streets raised me. The neighborhood dope man was my big brother, and I was my own father.

The Saga Continues

I picked up a few bad habits and generational curses from growing up in such a hostile environment. At age eleven I started using marijuana and alcohol, which opened the door to more demonic addictions. At the age of fourteen, I started using cocaine, and then quickly developed a heroin addiction at the age of sixteen. Heroin is one of the most addictive drugs out there, even more addictive than crack cocaine. Like any powerful stronghold, if someone tries to quit cold turkey it will cause dramatic effects, both mentally and physically.

Through my teenage years, I developed a criminal lifestyle. I stole cars, I robbed people, and I broke into their homes. I had shoot-outs with rival gangs and developed the reputation of a person you didn't want to mess with. I was arrested many times, once for battery on a police officer. I was facing five years in prison for that charge because I had broken the officer arm and his jaw when he tried to apprehend me. But by the grace of God I beat those charges. Once the police realized I assaulted one of their own, I was a target. That night I was arrested, they beat me up pretty badly, but the doctors wrote something in the report that kind of helped me with my case. My mother put up the house for my bond, and even though I wasn't saved, I knew God had something to do with it.

My first supernatural encounter occurred when I was fourteen.

I was going to Mississippi for a family reunion. Before I left, a friend of mine told me I needed to slow down. He was referring to my habit of stealing cars and performing robberies. While in Mississippi, I met up with my cousins. We stole our relative's car and went for a joy ride. All of a sudden, we turned onto a red dirt road where this twenty to thirty foot cliff was. The car sped out of control, and off the cliff we went. As we were in the air, everything went into slow motion. The car finally landed on the ground, bounced several times, and hit a tree that split the hood of the car in half. My face went through the windshield. Glass sliced my eyelids in two, ripped flesh from my face, and cut my neck. After the collision, my face print was left on the windshield with a pair of bloody angel wings around it.

When they pulled the car out of the wreckage, it frightened everyone who saw it. What made it even stranger was the fact that I was the only one hurt in the car; everyone else left without a scratch. The doctors said that if I had turned my head slightly to the left or right when I went through the glass my head would have been cut clean off. Everyone said it was a miracle that we lived from such a wreck, but all I could think of was the bloody angel wings with my face print. That was the first supernatural encounter that I can remember, I knew from that accident that God was with me.

Let's fast forward a bit to when I was in my twenties. I was facing ninety-nine years in prison for armed robbery and attempted murder. I'd been involved in a shoot-out with a guy over money.

The event had made the papers. I was about to lose everything; my life was about to be over.

My Prison Encounter

When most people get locked up in prison, one of two things takes place: you either get into more trouble or find God. I didn't know anything about God, but I knew about church. My mother made me go to a traditional Baptist church while I was growing up. Each time I went to church, I automatically fall asleep. To this day, I believe it wasn't the devil that made me do that. I believe it was God's way of keeping my spirit man from feeding on, and digesting religious spirits.

Now, back to the story in prison. I met some guys who knew about Jesus. They would sing hymns and had a joy about them, even in the midst of their terrible situations. I had a choice to make: I could sit miserable in prison for the rest of my life, or I could find joy in the midst of my sorrow. So, I started attending their prayer meetings. I accepted Jesus as my savior, and my heroin addiction left me instantly. I suffered no withdrawal symptoms. It was like I was brand new!

I vowed to God that I would never touch heroin again if He got me out of prison. Instead, I would be fully devoted to serving Him. Well, God is a covenant keeper, and He got me out of prison. They reduced my attempted murder charge to assault with a deadly weapon; but then they let me go because there were no witnesses, and the defendant didn't even show up. With the arrest record I had, there was no way they were supposed to let me go that easy. My mother thought it was because of a letter she had sent to the judge, but it was actually my petition to the judge who lives up above that did it. Thank you, Jesus!

Breach of Contract

When I was released from prison, the first thing I did was kiss the ground and shout, "I am free!" Well, at least I thought I was. I was clean from drugs, but I still had old soul ties to my street family and to my neighborhood. I distanced myself from my friends for a season so I could remain on the right track and stay off drugs. But, I ended up developing a new habit, my music career.

My friend from the neighborhood was a straight-up guy. He and I started a record company called "Kings of the Round Table." It was a success! We were well known locally in the New Orleans underground circle, but we had no national status. By that time, I had three kids and a wife. I had already wasted many years pursuing aspirations of being the biggest kingpin gangster that ever lived. Now, I had once again put my family on the back burner, but this time it was to pursue a music career. In spite of their cries, I remained diligent in my chase of the American dream.

Just as I had found God in prison, I also left Him in there. The lifestyle I was leading could not co-exist with His plan and purpose for my life. It's hard being an angel when you're surrounded by devils. I went back to smuggling drugs, and in my own twisted imagination, I figured as long as I wasn't using them I was fine. My music was my new addiction, and I wasn't going to let anyone stop my dream. I was determined.

The Storm after My Storms

Hurricane Katrina hit the Gulf Coast of Louisiana in August 2005. It was a category-five storm with winds up to two hundred miles per hour. It breached the levies of the Crescent City. Gas prices skyrocketed and haven't really come down since. This storm damaged a lot of oil rigs in the gulf, and homes were under water. Thousands died in the flood, and many more died because of the late response of our government. Many women and children died because of dehydration and lack of food.

Many saw Hurricane Katrina as a catastrophic disaster of biblical proportions, and it was. It was God's judgment on a wicked city. Before the storm in New Orleans, the city had the highest murder rate in the United States. We had more murders than big cities like Los Angeles, Detroit, Chicago and New York. A lot of people call Las Vegas "Sin City," but Las Vegas had nothing on New Orleans, aka "The Big Easy." With its demonic heritage of the French connection, and voodoo possession origins, riverboat gambling and the Louisiana purchase of slaves. It also served as the first city where the Sicilian Mafia landed in America, they were called "the black hand" before they started the five-families in New York and Chicago. It all started in New Orleans. So, when others saw this storm as a tragedy, I saw it as an escape from Egypt. The pharaoh of this land was the economic and criminal justice system. It kept the people in bondage. Before Hurricane Katrina, studies showed that 85 percent of all African American males in the Orleans parish district would have been incarcerated more than fifteen times, and murdered by their twenty-fifth year of age. Where there is high poverty and low quality education, criminal activity will be high as well.

To the Promised Land

Many people from Louisiana migrated to Texas, mostly to the Houston and Dallas areas. I was separated from my wife and my music business partner during the storm. I went with my mother and children to Baton Rouge to escape. But then, I was able to get in touch with my partner in the music. He had fled to Houston and told me how we could make some money with the music and other things there. Although I was no longer on drugs, I still had a hustler mentality. So, once again I left my children to chase after a dream. Houston was like a gold mine. The women seemed more appealing, the drug dealers looked weaker, and I was a predator on the prowl. I thought I had hit it big, but I was in for a big surprise.

The Game Is Not the Same

Several hustlers from New Orleans came with the same mentality they had in the Big Easy, "If you don't give it, we will take it." But, Houston had a rude awakening for those people. The drug dealers had already heard of the New Orleans' people's reputation for murdering and robbery, so a lot of conflict arose. The guys from Houston refused to cut us in on the drug trade, so the war began. The media started to refer to New Orleans evacuees as "refugees," like we were from a different country or from a far-away land. This fueled the anger of a lot of New Orleans natives. We were being profiled as animals, not just from a certain race, but also from other minority groups, including our own African-American community.

The murder rate increased in Houston, and violence broke out in the schools, not just among the kids from New Orleans, but also with the kids from Houston. That city's drug dealers committed crimes, knowing that the police department would blame the evacuees from New Orleans. It was a disaster, and I was in the middle of it. It seemed like the promised land" wasn't as promising as I had thought. That spirit of murder, drug selling, and other vices had followed me from New Orleans. I had left the land of Egypt, but it seemed like the pharaoh mentality wouldn't let my people go! I was still a slave to my self-afflicted bondage.

My Conversion

What is a conversion? The word conversion means "the act or state of changing to adopt new opinions or beliefs." In Houston, I had started a prostitution ring, making women sell their bodies for money. I was also selling drugs on the side to pay rent and to keep my music company afloat. My friend Joel, was doing the same thing. After a while, he and I had a falling out and parted ways. My music dreams were dashed. Joel kept pursuing music without me.

I was focused on finding a way to come up and take over Houston. I had all the women, cars, drugs, and guns that I wanted, but I still felt empty on the inside. I lost the relationship I'd had with my kids in New Orleans. I was separated from the wife I had at the time. I had really hit rock bottom; I was only surviving off temporary satisfaction.

A New Friend

Joel and I were really close friends before the storm came along. We sold drugs together, robbed together, and made music together before we had the falling out. Losing friendship with him was a big blow to me. If there was anybody that would have my back forever, I figured it would have been him. With Joel out of picture. I trusted no one. My heart grew colder by the day.

One day, I heard a knock on my front door. To my surprise, it was Joel. Part of me wanted to kill him, but I still had love for him as a brother. This time, something was different about him. He told me he'd gotten saved and that he was turning his life around. I'd had an encounter with God before in jail, but most people do. When they get out, it's like that encounter never happened. But something was different about Joel's conversion. He was humble and his face looked brighter. He even talked in a softer tone. That wasn't Joel at all! I had a "new" friend.

The Power of the Word

Joel walked into my house as a new man. But, I had heard all this Jesus stuff before from church people, my wife, and others, and I didn't want to hear it again. I felt like I had breached my contract with God and I'd just mess up again. Plus, I was entrenched so deeply in sin. How could I change? I was convinced that God couldn't forgive a murderer, pimp, drug dealer, and thief like me.

As Joel talked, he didn't preach to me about my sins. The Holy Spirit knew I would judge Joel for his past and not receive Him because of it. So He did something very wise. He told Joel to have me read 2 Timothy 3:1–7 out loud:

> *"This know also, that in the last days perilous times shall come. For men shall be lovers of their own selves, covetous, boasters, proud, blasphemers, disobedient to parents, unthankful, unholy, Without natural affection, trucebreakers, false accusers, incontinent, fierce despisers of those that are good, Traitors, heady, high-minded, lovers of pleasures, more than lovers of God; Having a form of godliness, but denying the power thereof: from such turn away. For of this sort are they which creep into houses, and lead captive silly women laden with sins, led away with divers lusts. Ever learning and never able to come to the knowledge of the truth."*

Then Joel said, "Now tell me, where do you find yourself in that Scripture?"

All of a sudden, a heavy feeling of conviction fell over me. I begin to weep and said, "I can't find anything in that Scripture that doesn't describe me" I was the whole chapter! Then, I fell on my knees and felt an electricity travel all over my body. I cried for hours on the floor and gave my life over to Jesus Christ. I was done. I started giving away my cars and jewelry. I told the women I was pimping that I quit. I flushed all the drugs I had down the toilet, and all leftover addictions left me instantly.

I had done everything possible to succeed in life, but all those ventures had fallen through. When I was finally "arrested" by the Holy Spirit, I knew I was going to be a prisoner of Christ forever. I was free, but under a new and better yoke. This was different from my prison experience. In prison, I just wanted freedom so I could go back to the streets. Now, I just wanted freedom from sin. I was really born again.

After my conversion, many people at my job and apartment complex were also saved and delivered. We would pray for people, and instant conviction would fall upon them. The managers at my job were afraid to write me up when I was late for work, because they believed God would get them if they did. People were filled instantly with the Holy Spirit, and they spoke in tongues. It was glorious. People in my apartment building referred to it as the Westridge Revival. I had finally discovered the most important piece in the puzzle of life. Thank you, Jesus, for saving my soul.

On March 3, 2008, Shawn Anthony Morris was reborn!

—◊—

I pray in the name of Jesus Christ that every person who reads this testimony will be born again, set free, and delivered! Lord, according to Revelation 12:11, "And they overcame him by the blood of the Lamb, and by the word of their testimony: and they loved not their lives unto death." In Jesus name I pray, that every over comer who speaks his or her testimony receives power from on high to destroy the enemy camp, and receive recompense for everything that was stolen from him or her. In Jesus mighty name, it is done.

Chapter 5
The Health Principle

Health Versus Healing

I am not a medical practitioner, but I do study health and wholeness biblically, and through medical information I can glean from. I cannot claim that any remedy, product, or natural substance I suggest will cure, heal, or prevent any disease. My intention is to guide you and give you key steps, hoping to lead you to a healthier lifestyle.

Modern day Christianity focuses a lot on receiving healing from a sovereign touch from Jesus. I am a healing evangelist. I hold healing crusades in the United States and abroad, so I fully believe that the supernatural power of God can heal the sick. However, as I take this journey to see the world, and the body of Christ, made whole, I've asked myself: what's the root cause of these illnesses? Is it the devil? The Holy Spirit answered me, "*No, it is not satan. He only uses humans' lack of knowledge about protecting my temple.*"

I thought, "*What temple?*" Then the Scripture popped up in my spirit: "*Know ye not that **ye are the temple of God**, and that the Spirit of God dwelleth in you? **If any man defile the temple of God**, him shall **God destroy**; for the temple of God is holy, which temple ye are*" 1 Corinthians 3:16–17 (emphasis added). This states that God shall destroy, not the devil. So we must stop blaming the devil for our infirmities. What goes on the inside of God's temple, which is our body, is our responsibility. The devil just takes advantage of our ignorance.

The Holy Spirit made a joke one day. He said, "Shawn, you know why satan is the accuser of the brethren?"

I said, "No, why?"

He said, "Because the brethren keep accusing him."

I laughed for days about that. The Holy Spirit was saying that the blame must be shifted so we can see transformation and results. If someone who is filled with the Spirit of God, speaks in tongues, has faith to move mountains, and is constantly praying for the removal of sickness, yet nothing happens, then I propose it is not a demon, but an unhealthy lifestyle. Let me give you an example. There was a woman who came into our meeting with diabetes mellitus, which is a disorder of the pancreas where the body fails to produce an adequate amount of insulin, the substance that metabolizes carbohydrates and regulates sugar levels in the blood. This woman came to one of our healing meetings, and the power of God hit her like a Mack truck. She went back to the doctor and discovered that her insulin levels, blood pressure, and other stats were normal. She was healed!

Several months passed, and she came back to our meetings looking sicker than she had the last time she came.

I asked the Lord why she had not kept her healing. The Lord showed me that the lady was still eating large amounts of sugars, starches, and fats. The "real spirit" that caused her disease was bad eating habits. If we take full responsibility for our part in the up-keep of God's temple, then we will be compelled to change our lifestyles.

What's Health?

Health is "an overall sound condition of a living organism" or "freedom from disease." One of the Hebrew words translated as "health" is *arukah*, meaning health in the sense of "restoring to soundness or wholeness." Figuratively speaking it implies "to be made perfect."

Father God created us to be perfect beings. *"Be ye therefore perfect, even as your Father which is in heaven is perfect"* (Matthew 5:48). This indicates we must be like God Himself. Genesis 1:26 tells us, *"And God said, Let us make man in our image, after our likeness."* What is an image? An image is a likeness or a semblance of someone or something. So, we see here that God imagined us to look like Him.

In the book of John, we read that no man has seen God (1:18). But in John 14:9, we read of a conversation between Jesus and Philip:

> *"Philip said unto him, Lord **show us the Father**, and it sufficeth us. Jesus saith unto him, Have I been so long time with you, and yet hast thou not known me, Philip? **he that hath seen me have seen the Father**; and how sayest thou then, Show us the Father?"* [Emphasis added].

Jesus stated that if you have seen Him, you have seen the Father. Remember what Colossians 2:9 says about Jesus, *"For in Him dwelleth all the fullness of the Godhead bodily."* Jesus was the perfect example of the image of God. The Holy Spirit is changing us into His image, as it tells us in 2 Corinthians 3:18: *"But we all, with open face beholding as in a glass the glory of the Lord, **are changed into the same image** from glory to glory, even as by the Spirit of the Lord."* (emphasis added).

Now regarding God's physical image, I have seen posters, banners, wooden graven images, and all sorts of paraphernalia with Jesus on the cross. I notice that most of these images portray Jesus with perfect abs, chiseled features, and a strong chin. We don't know if these images accurately reflect His features. What we do know is that when Jesus was on earth, He walked many miles, He fasted often, He also went on a three and a half year journey of intense ministry, with hardly any rest. So we can probably assume He was in really good shape.

The Lord wants us to be healthy and shapely. Another Hebrew word translated as "health" is *marpe*. It means "medicine or a cure," "deliverance," "remedy," or "sound and wholesome." To me, the word "deliverance" stood out the most in this definition of health. Health is deliverance. The Greek meaning of deliverance is "*aphesis*," which means "forgiveness," "pardon," or "freedom." Health is freedom from the limitations this fallen world has put on us. It is a pardon from the prison of sickness and infirmity. Once we are released from prison, we must not commit crimes against the temple (body) that will put us back in prison of sickness.

There are many people, especially Christians, who don't let anything through the gates of their eyes and ears through music or television, but they open the door to the enemy through the mouth with an unhealthy diet. I tell people all the time, "When you are sick, stop and ask God to heal His body, because the violation was done to Christ, not us." We simply suffer the effects of this dilemma, because we are His body. It hurts the Lord more than it hurts us when we are sick, because it's His body that's getting sick, not just ours. Let's T.A.P. and see what we can do to prevent such grievance against the Holy Spirit temple.

Health through Fasting

I would like to thank Patricia and Paul Bragg for the wonderful information I gleaned from their book *The Miracle of Fasting: Proven Throughout History for Physical, Mental, & Spiritual Rejuvenation*, published in 2004 by Health Science in Santa Barbara, California.

Fasting is abstinence from food and drink for a period of time. It is frequently mentioned in the Scriptures. The only official fast the Lord required was the Day of Atonement. Religious fasting was mainly observed in order to express mourning for sin.

However fasts were not necessarily religious. They were common when someone was suffering grief, vexation, or anxiety for any reason. Oftentimes, people fasted when someone near and dear to them died. An example was after Saul and Jonathan died: "*And they took their bones, and buried them under a tree at Jabesh, and fasted seven days*" (1 Samuel 31:13). The Gospels tell us that fasting was customary for those who desired to lead a special religious or spiritual lifestyle. Luke 2:37 describes a prophetess named Anna: "*And she was a widow of about fourscore and four years, which departed not from the temple, **but served God with fasting** and prayers night and day.*" (emphasis added). When you fast, it is a service to the Lord.

Being a servant is more than just doing ministry work. It also requires taking care of the temple of God, which is the physical body. Romans 12:1 mentions this duty: "*I beseech you therefore brethren, by the mercies of God, that **ye present your bodies as a living sacrifice**, holy, acceptable unto God, which is **your reasonable service**.*" [Emphasis added]. The Greek word for "reasonable" in this verse is **logikos**, meaning "rational or logical." The Holy Spirit told me one day, "*You must starve so they can eat.*" I understood that my lack of fasting was keeping others from receiving from God. What a responsibility! Fasting is our anatomy's way of removing pathological conditions from our bodies. It accomplishes the same thing for us psychologically which is the (soul) and spiritually which is the (spirit). Roman 12:1 also states: **Present your bodies as a living sacrifice, holy, acceptable unto God**... See you can not accept anything from God, until your first acceptable, and the only way to do that, is by becoming a living sacrifice, through fasting. The scriptures emphasis it's *a living sacrifice,* so this tells us that we are not going to die in this sacrificial process. God does not want us to kill ourselves in fasting, but wants us to spring clean the temple he dwells in, and remove all unwanted guest in our inner kingdom.

Fasting Health Benefits

Fasting requires discipline. It is often spoken of in the Old Testament as "*afflicting the soul*" (Leviticus 23:27). Those who fasted frequently dressed in sackcloth, tore their clothes, put ashes on their heads, and walked barefoot. They sacrificed their personal will to get God's attention.

But, fasting isn't only for spiritual or mental benefit. It also yields physical benefits. Fasting detoxifies the body and allows it to rejuvenate and energize at the cellular level. It removes excess free radicals from cells and boosts the immune system. The process of fasting is basically self-digestion. During the cleansing process of a fast, the body intuitively decomposes and burns only damaged or diseased tissues (such as abscesses or tumors) or unneeded substances (such as excess fat deposits, excess water, or congestive wastes). Sometimes, there are dramatic changes when these wastes are expelled.

Sickness is merely the body's indication that it needs to be detoxified. It's the body's "check engine" light to warn us of accumulated poisons and toxins. Fasting helps rid our bodies of sickness by stabilizing our pH levels and eliminating toxic materials we have ingested through unhealthy eating and drinking, or via environmental pollutions. The foods we eat and our environment all tend to promote an acidic state. Fasting helps alkalize the body. Diseases thrive in an acidic environment while alkalinity promotes health.

Let's point out what fasting is not. Fasting is not refraining from watching television for a couple of days or staying off the computer for a week. I have heard people speak of fasting from wrong thinking or speaking filthy language. That is not fasting, that's getting rid of bad habits.

In the New Testament the Greek word *nestis*, translated as "fasting," means "not eating" or "abstinence from food." So if you're not abstaining from food, then you're not fasting. When you fast, you give your organs a break from digestion and all the processes the body undergoes as a result of that. Fasting is a key constituent in revitalizing health. It also increases sensory perception, so it will often sharpen your mind and make your body, soul, and spirit more alert.

Let's begin to incorporate the fasting principle in our everyday lives not just for spiritual purposes, but also for the health benefits it brings to our bodies. As we fast, Isaiah 58:8 promises us, "*Then shall **thy light break forth as the morning,** and **thine health shall spring forth speedily**: and thy righteousness shall go before thee; **the glory of the Lord shall be thy reward.**"* (emphasis added). That promise alone is worth fasting. So lets T.A.P.

Bless Food

There are many different ways to achieve vital health. Many people spend thousands of dollars a year on weight-loss solutions and gym membership fees, but rarely go to the gym. Those who go to the gym faithfully still may not see the results they are looking for. So, as time progresses, they may stop taking the diet pills and begin to cut back on their gym attendance.

But, there is one thing that humans can't stop doing, and that's eating. The food industry is a trillion dollar a year market. It has been said that whoever controls the food, controls the world. We can live without computers, gold, copper, iron, and various other elements. But, no nation, government, or human being can go without food.

In Psalm 103, the psalmist is blessing the Lord for the good things in his life. Verse five reads: "*Who satisfieth thy **mouth with good things**; so that thy **youth is renewed** like the eagle's.*" (emphasis added). *Thy mouth with good things* is talking about food. David is pointing out that God would bless the food, and in His doing that, physical health would be renewed back to its youthful, energized state. Verse one says, "*Bless the Lord, O my soul: and all that is within me, bless his holy name.*" The writer separated the "soul" realm from another realm by using the word ***and***. To figure out the other realm he was referring to, we must first explore what the soulish realm consists of. The soul is the mind, will, and emotions of a human being. With that understanding of what the soul is, there could be only two other realms the writer was talking about when he made the statement, ***all that is within me.***" The only two realms left in a three-part being of a human, are the spiritual and physical realms. I feel that this Scripture was showcasing the depths of all that was in his physical being, as well as his spiritual and soulish counterparts. The writer wanted the Lord to bless his mind and emotions, but also his food so his physical body could remain sharp.

Exodus 23:25 reads, "*And ye shall serve the Lord your God, and He shall **bless thy bread**, and the **water**; and I will take **sickness away from*** *the midst of thee.*" (emphasis added). According to this Scripture, the Lord will bless our bread and water, and sickness will be removed from us as well. The Lord is giving us a motive to seek and serve Him with a healthy diet and eating habits. Most Americans eat a great deal of red meat, doughnuts, coffee, soda, hamburgers, and pizza. These foods are acidic and not good for optimal health. The Lord has furnished the earth with plenty of alkaline foods and liquids to keep us healthy in this fallen world. These foods stimulate nerves and other tissues in the body. They fuel the brain and other vital organs, such as the heart. So, with that being said, let's clean the temple!

For optimal results items in the following list should be organic.

Alkaline vegetables: amaranth, asparagus, beets, broccoli, bell peppers, cabbage, carrots, cauliflower, celery, chard, chayote, collard greens, cucumbers, dandelion greens, eggplant, garbanzo beans, garlic, green peas, jicama, kale, lettuce, mushrooms, mustard greens, okra, olives, onions, pumpkin, quinoa, radishes, spinach, string beans, sweet potatoes, turnip greens, and zucchini, to name a few.

Alkaline fruits: apples, apricots, avocadoes, bananas, berries, cantaloupe, cherries, dates, figs, grapes, grapefruit, lemons, limes, mangos, melons, nectarines, oranges, papayas, peaches, pears, pineapples, plums or prunes, raisins, strawberries, tangerines, tomatoes, and tropical fruits, to name a few.

It is important to eat these fruits and vegetables raw or not overcook them. Cooking destroys enzymes in the foods that assist with digestion. Preserving the enzymes helps us to digest our food properly, which maximizes the assimilation of nutrients. Also, remember that the body is made up of 75 percent water, so if we fix the water problem we will fix the body issues. Our water should be alkaline and purified by reverse osmosis.

Consider this thought: if we learn to consume the right produce, revival may break out in our churches because the healing lines will be much shorter. And, our thoughts will be much clearer to hear from God. So get healthy and T.A.P.

—⁓—

Father, right now I pray in the name of your Holy Son, Jesus Christ, that every person who reads this prayer receives conviction for wrong eating habits, wrong mindsets, and traditional strongholds. Bless their bread and water, and take sickness from them in the mighty name of Jesus Christ. T.A.P.!

Chapter 7
Breaking the Invisible Walls

In this chapter, I will discuss some issues that need to be addressed in the body of Christ and the world. Some may be offended, but others will take this as a spiritual wake up call.

What Walls?

What invisible walls am I talking about? Well, first let me explain what these terms mean. The word invisible means "not capable of being seen," "not visible," or "hidden." If there is a "wall" that most people cannot see or recognize, it's because that wall is used to be an invisible force, that blinds their intellect and spiritual discernment. Its main purpose is to be a snare for their integrity. A wall is a vertical structure used to separate or enclose an area. When there is a wall in your life, it is closing in a certain area of your life. Nothing can come in, and nothing can go out. It's a structure that structures your life.

Now, this structure whether put up by you, your environment, social influence, your cultural back-ground, or an unknown entity that has limited your capabilities. Your capacity, which is the total amount of data or information that can be processed, stored, or generated, is now hindered. A Hebrew word translated as "wall" is *cheyl*, which can mean "entrenchment." Entrenchment means "to dig a trench or hole for the purpose of defense." So, when you put a wall up, you have a defensive spirit that is digging holes into your inner man.

In 1 Thessalonians 5:23, we read: *"And the very God of peace sanctify you wholly; and I pray God your **whole spirit** and **soul** and **body** be **preserved blameless** unto the coming of our Lord Jesus Christ."* (emphasis added). Wow! If a wall is an entrenchment that digs holes in your inner man because of a defensive spirit, this means the whole man is affected. Your spirit must be whole, not having holes. If there are holes in your spirit, you can no longer be blameless before the Lord. Consequently, due to the disarray of the spirit man because of this wall, your body and soul will be affected as well, and you limit your access to the heavens.

Some of you might still be asking the question, "What walls?" Well, let's T.A.P. and uncover the forces that are keeping the body of Christ, and the world, from being preserved blameless before the Lord—whole in spirit, soul, and body.

The Racial Wall

I will touch on a subject that has been one of the main walls of separation since the beginning of time. The wall I speak of has a spirit of apathy and indifference that has divided nations, families, and God's children for generations. This wall is hidden by ignorance, denial, and negligence. This is the wall of racism. Racism is the thought or belief that one race or culture is better or superior to another race or culture. The racism wall stems from the spirit of division.

I believe this spirit of division was the first spirit that took over Lucifer the archangel, causing him to grow prideful and eventually; fall from Heaven. Pride was Lucifer's main issue, but I believe that pride was birthed out of the spirit of division. This spirit led to the first racial war between the angels who stayed faithful to God and the angels who followed Lucifer (satan) and became demons. Before demons were demons, they were angels. Most people have different opinions about this subject, but the truth of the matter is that Lucifer (satan) was an angel until he rebelled against God. When you have a spirit of racism, you become something demonic, just like Lucifer. And, when the spirit of division comes into play, the separation between different groups begins.

So, racism was here before the creation of man.

When man was formed, God created a garden for him, and in that garden was a tree of the knowledge of good and evil. Within that knowledge was an understanding of the spirit of division, or racism that was in heaven before Lucifer's fall. That tree was God's reminder of the betrayal that took place in the heavens with another one of His created beings, the angels. Genesis 2:16–17 says:

> *"And the LORD God commanded the man saying, Of every tree in the garden thou may freely eat: But of the tree of the* **knowledge of good and evil,** *thou shall not eat of it: for in the day that thou eatest thereof **thou shalt surely die**."* *[Emphasis added.]*

What is this knowledge of good and evil? The word knowledge in the New Testament is often translated from the Greek word **epignosis**, which means "knowledge," "perception," or "discernment." Discernment or discerning of spirits, is one of the gifts of

94

the Holy Spirit listed in 1 Corinthians 12:10. Knowledge is a gift of the Spirit that recognizes, perceives, or discerns a spirit, whether it is good or evil. Here is my point: God did not want us to recognize, perceive, or discern that spirit of division, which is the mother of racism. God understood that, once we discern or recognize that spirit, we could become partakers of its fruit. The curiosity of man's free will loves to challenge the rules of authority, because it has freedom of choice. This is what the Lord tried to protect us from in the garden. This was also the main thing satan tries to make us recognize.

Genesis 3:5 says: *"For God doth know that in the day ye eat thereof, then **your eyes shall be opened**, and ye shall be as gods, **knowing good and evil.**"* {Emphasis added}. The devils tactic was to get Eve to use her spiritual eyes to recognize that spirit of division. Once she recognize the difference, her free will began to lust after the forbidden things of God. After the sin was committed it caused a separation between the Creator and His creation, which stem from the spirit of division. Then man was force out of the garden because of it (see Genesis 3:24).

I can go through the Bible and point out historical examples of the war of racism: Sarah and Hagar, Isaac and Ishmael, Egyptians and Jews, Jews and Gentiles, and the list goes on and on. That spirit has been the reason for conflict in the Middle East and across the globe since the beginning of time. The body of Christ must break the wall of racism, or we will never see renewal, revival, or a great awakening. The wealth transfer that many people speak about will not happen until this wall is broken down for good. Proverbs 13:22 tells us, *"The wealth of the sinner is stored up for the righteous"* (NKJV). But if we, the body of Christ, are "sinners," from the Hebrew word ***chata*** meaning "to miss the way or forfeit," then the great wealth transfer will not happen, it will be forfeited.

When there is a diverse crowd of people, and one race is sitting together with their own race, as I start my meeting, I politely ask everyone to get out of their chairs and sit next to someone of a different racial group, until we look like Neapolitan ice cream or Oreo cookies. If we don't mix the cultures and races, we indicate to God that we are still eating from the tree of knowledge of good and evil, which breeds the spirit of division the mother of racism! I urge you don't get kicked out of your garden of Eden, because you choose to continue still eating from this tree.

With that being said, I believe that God will not pour out His Spirit on an all-black church, an all-white church, or even an all-Spanish or all-Asian Church. I believe that when all nations are assembled, just like in Acts chapter two, when all nations and tribes heard their native tongues being spoken, then the last great move of God's Spirit will take place, before the return of the Messiah Jesus. Acts chapter two is a prophetic shadow of what's to come. So get prepared, break this wall today, and T.A.P.!

Social Status Wall

Another invisible wall that is just as poisonous as the wall of racism is the wall of Social Status. This particular wall has no racial, cultural, economic, denominational, or ethnic barriers. It thrives off human and earthly desires and focuses on material gain. These things have nothing to do with building the Kingdom. The world has been dealt an injustice by those who have stuffed the current images of ideal social status and popular lifestyles into our psyches. There is a burden on mankind to live up to the standards of public opinion that very few can obtain. This in turn, causes people to become social rejects.

The Lord wants to give us our heart's desires, as long as they do not take our focus away from Kingdom business. Matthew 6:33 states: "*But seek ye first the **kingdom of God**, and **his righteousness**; and all these things shall be added unto you.*" [Emphasis added]. Kingdom business and God's righteousness should be "top priority," properly and in accordance with recognized principles. Seeking the Kingdom first is the anointed principle of T.A.P.ing into the glory and have your needs and wants met. We must get into a position in order to receive our possessions.

Today, we seek the latest trends, fashions, styles, technology gadgets, and gimmicks while the Kingdom suffers in a tremendous way. What the body of Christ doesn't understand is that you can be a social guru according to society but be a social misfit according to God's standards. I am not advertising that God does not want us to have material blessings or even worldly friends. Jesus did say in Luke 16:9, "*And I say unto you, Make to yourselves friends of the mammon of unrighteousness.*" You can have friends from the world, but not be a friend of the world. Trust me there is a difference.

That's why Jesus also stated in Matthew 5:29, "*And if the right eye offend thee; pluck it out, and cast it from thee: for it is profitable for thee that one of thy members should perish, and not that thy whole body should be cast into hell.*" Therefore, if your social life is causing you to sin willfully, cut it out! It is not profiting you in any way. Don't allow your personal life to affect your spiritual life. When you are affected by society, you are ineffective with God.

This wall has led to the shutdown of many churches, simply because they are "on the wrong side of town. Other pastors and churches refuse to help those ministries because they are deemed unsuitable by society's point of view. But, I always say, "Know them by their fruit, not by their suit." Men and women can't find suitable mates because society says, "He must make this much money," and, "She must have a figure like this." Unholy concern over the body image is the cause of anorexia nervosa, a disorder seen primarily in adolescent girls, which is characterized by prolonged refusal to eat, extreme weight loss, and an abnormal fear of being obese. Thousands of girls die each year because of this invisible wall society has built around self-image. God wants us to have recognition and material wealth, but He doesn't want us to steal, sleep around, fall into depression, or starve ourselves to death in order to get those things. Break the social status wall and be a true world changer, be different, be yourself and T.A.P.!

The Economic Wall

The Economic wall is the third anointing killer and surely the most deadly of the walls discussed in this chapter. Economics is the science relating to the development, production, and management of material wealth. A biblical view of economics is found in Deuteronomy 8:18: "*But thou shall remember the LORD thy God; for it is He that giveth thee power to get wealth.*" I used to wonder how, and why would God do this for someone like me.

Before I made Jesus the Lord of my life, I had the common world mentality that education, social status, high-paying jobs, and hard work would get me wealth. When I received the Lord into my life, I rejected that worldly mentality, and figured that Jesus wanted me to live poor in order to live holy. I didn't quite understand how or why He would give me the "***power to get wealth***" when I was supposed to be poor. The rest of the eighteenth verse in Deuteronomy 8 tells us why He wanted me wealthy: "*That He may establish His covenant which He swore unto thy fathers, as it is this day.*" God has developed an economic system called "His covenant." It's through this covenant that we receive our material necessities for life and success.

The economic wall has grown higher throughout the years. The epidemic has become catastrophic in the period between the nineteenth and twenty-first centuries. Oftentimes, pastors, evangelists, prophets, and revivalists refused to come to meetings or services unless there is an honorarium. They wanted to know how many people would fit in the church, so they could know what the offering would potentially be. The Lord did "*ordained that they which preach the gospel should live of the gospel*" (1 Corinthians 9:14). It is also true that "*if we have sown unto you spiritual things, is it a great thing if we shall reap your carnal things?*" (1 Corinthians 9:11). Yes, it costs to do the work of ministry.

However, Paul also wrote in 1 Corinthians 9:16: "*For though I preach the gospel, I have nothing to glory of: for necessity is laid upon me; yea, woe is unto me, if I preach not the gospel.*" See, I believe there is woe unto those itinerant ministers who refuse to come to a city, nation, or church because of the lack of a promise, that they will receive an adequate offering. The Lord Himself told us to "*heal the sick, cleanse the lepers, raise the dead, cast out devils, freely ye have received freely give. Provide neither gold, nor silver, nor brass in your purses, Nor scrip for your journey, neither two coats, neither shoes, nor yet slaves; for the worker is worthy of his meat [wages]*" (Matthew 10:8–10). Let me break down what the Lord Jesus was commissioning the disciples and us to do.

The reason men cannot freely give, it's because they have not freely received. The key word here is *free*, in a sense of "I am free and not indebted to you because it was given to me freely."

The struggles of traditional ministries have led the church to put a price tag on the Gospel. Pastors and leaders have taken the focus from the development and discipleship of souls, to the development and growth of the church structure. They are focused on, funding buildings, and increasing membership. Jesus said to make disciples (Matthew 28:19), not church members. Matthew 10:9 says not to bring anything, and verse ten says that "*the worker is worthy of his meat [wages]*." It's sad to say, but we, as the body, barely perform verse eight ("*Heal the sick, cleanse the lepers, raise the dead, and cast out devils*"), yet we expect a Matthew 10:10 return of wages. If you're not fully supplying verse eight, then please don't expect the verse ten harvest. You must prove yourself worthy of your wages. So let's T.A.P. by breaking down the economic wall!

False Identity Wall

What is an identity? Logically it is the make up of who you are as a person. According to Webster's Dictionary, the meaning of the word identity is "the condition or state of being a specific person or thing that's recognizable as such," or "the condition or fact of being the same as something." Now that's a strong definition.

There are several key points of the definition that stick out. First is the condition or state of being a specific person. What is your condition? A condition is the mode or state of existence of a person, thing, or circumstance. Whatever mode or state of mind you are in, that is what you will become. The Scriptures even states, "*As he thinketh in his heart, so is he*" (Proverbs 23:7). You will determine your future by the way you process data.

Since our state of mind determines our future, let's begin to change our future. Here is another scripture reference: "*And be not conformed to this world: but be ye transformed by the **renewing of your*** *mind, that ye may **prove what is that good**, and **acceptable**, and **perfect**, will of God*" (Romans 12:2, emphasis added).

Before we can renew our minds with the truth, we must first break down the invisible wall of false identity. The body of Christ has been infected with a false humility doctrine. The following statements are common, but have their basis in the unbiblical, false humility doctrine. Please realize that if you have made these statements, it is not your fault. They stem from traditions of religious, social, and cultural defects.

I had nothing to do with it, it was all God.

God gets all the glory.

I am nothing, He is everything.

In one sense, these statements are true because God is everything. However, by demeaning our own identities, we are giving the body of Christ a defeated mind set. Let's begin with this statement, "**God gets all the glory.**" This statement is true, but in a sense, it is also false. Romans 8:16–17 says, "*The **Spirit itself** beareth witness with **our spirit** that we are **the children of God**: And if children, then heirs; **heirs of God**, and **joint-heirs with Christ**; if so be that **we suffer with him**, that **we may be also glorified together**"* (emphasis added). Wow! This verse gives the body of Christ their identification verification. It does not say all glory goes to God or is taken from God, but it does state man's role in God's dealings in the earth realm. Most people (particularly religious people) would say, "Well, you're not Jesus!" Well, according to Scripture I am part of Jesus body, the body of Christ (Ephesians 5:30). No one walks separated from his body. So, in that sense, we are Jesus, at less a part of Him.

In John 14:20 Jesus says, "*At that day ye shall know that **I am in the Father**, and **ye in me**, and **I in you**.*" (emphasis added). A lot of us have grasped the concept of Jesus in us, but we haven't come to the understanding that we are also in Him. That is why in John 15:7 Jesus said, "***If ye abide in me**, and **my words abide in you**, ye shall ask what ye will, and it shall be done unto you.*" (emphasis added). This stresses once again not only that Jesus is in us, but that we are in Him.

Jesus is the living Word inside of us, but we are also a living word inside of Him. In the beginning God created with His words. He spoke the world into existence (Psalm 33:6, 9). The words God spoke became living beings. We came from God's insides. Genesis 1:27 tells us clearly, "*So God **created man in his own image**, in the image of God created he him; **male** and **female** created he them*" (emphasis added). God planted a word seed in mother earth and blew His breath into it, and mankind was born. Remember, we are also a word that was made flesh.

You may still be wrestling with the "you're not Jesus" part. Even if that's true, can we at least say we have the same access, rights, and anointing as Him? Romans 8:17 states this very clearly: "*And if children, then heirs; heirs of God, and joint-heirs with Christ.*" The body of Christ has trouble walking in son-ship because they don't have the revelation of this passage. We are heirs of God. An heir is a person who will inherit another's property or title. The Scripture says we are joint-heirs with Christ. It is similar to a husband and wife who share a joint bank account. One party has as much access to the account as the other.

Once again, the word heir means "a person who inherits another's **property** or **title**." Since we are joint-heirs with Christ, is it safe to say that, we share the title of *Christ* as well? I sense in the spirit that the false-humility spirit wants to rise up and stone me. To back up my theory, Psalm 105:15 says, "*Touch not mine **anointed ones** and do my prophets no harm*" (emphasis added). The Scripture says "anointed ones" that's plural not singular. There is more than one Christ (anointed one) according to this Scripture. We are joint-heirs; that means we have the same property and title as Christ.

Having this understanding will boost your faith level and confidence of who you are in God. When this happens, you will be able to access the miracles from heaven on earth because you too are an anointed one of God. Jesus is my big Brother and my King, but I am also a king. Revelation 1:6 tells us, "[Jesus Christ] *hath **made us kings** and **priests** unto His God and Father.*" (emphasis added) The body of Christ has received the priestly anointing but is lagging behind in the kingly anointing. Our hearts and minds must shift to accept both positions. The priestly anointing allows people to receive from the Lord, but the kingly anointing allows people to walk as the Lord. A cop and a robber can both have a gun, but it's the one with a badge of authority that makes the other one surrender. The difference is the cop is connected to the government (Kingdom) of that city or country while the robber has limited rights. The only right he has is the right to "remain silent". Get it !

We must display our Kingdom authority and arrest (bind) the enemy and thief. The reason Jesus is called "*King of kings and Lord of lords*" (Revelation 19:16) is that there are other kings and other lords. Therefore, God does not mind us defining ourselves as kings and lords.

In fact, Peter encourages us to identify and address each other as such: "*Even as Sara obeyed Abraham, **calling him lord**; whose daughters ye are, as long as, **ye do well** and are **not afraid with any terror***" (1 Peter 3:6, emphasis added). The verses before this speaks of holy women of old, and how they respected, addressed, and honored their husbands. The apostle Peter emphasized that this principle of honor must be practiced if one is to be considered a holy woman or man. When a man's manhood or title goes unacknowledged, or if it is degraded it is difficult for the "king" in that man to rise up and perform the duties of his title. Without the crown of glory on his head, and submission from others, a king is not entitled to bear that title.

Another belief contributing to the false identity wall is: "**all of God and none of me.**" Again, we have a statement that is true but not true. John 14:12 says, "*Verily, verily, I say unto you, He that believeth on me, **the works that I do shall he also**; and **greater works** than these **shall he do**; because I go unto my Father.*" (emphasis added). Jesus acknowledges in this passage that we will be the ones doing the work, and even greater works than He did. The Lord wants us to understand and acknowledge the vital roles we play as we participate in the working of miracles. The Lord doesn't want us to be on the sidelines cheerleading while He's playing in the game. Unless the quarterback has an offensive lineman, receiver, or running back to pass the ball to, the team can't get a touchdown. Teamwork makes the dream work.

Mark 16:20 says, "*And they went forth, and preached everywhere, the Lord **working with them**, and confirming the word with signs following*" (emphasis added). Remember, the Lord worked **with** them, not **for** them. The Holy Spirit is called the "helper" (John 14:26) because you're the one who has to do the work; He just helps.

The Bible says in Luke 2:52, "*Jesus **increased in wisdom** and stature, and **favor with God and man**.*" (emphasis added). Through increased wisdom, Jesus obtained favor not only with God but also with man. You need both. Being favored by God alone isn't enough

104

to do Kingdom work here on earth. Not understanding the importance of favor with man in our Christian walk has hindered the
flow of the Spirit for centuries. The Bible says in Acts 2:43, "*And
fear came upon every soul: and **many wonders** and **signs** were **done by the
apostles.**" (emphasis added). The apostles performed the signs and
wonders. Jesus said on the cross that His work was finished (John
19:30). So, it is our job to do the work now, not Jesus.

This notion is clarified in 1 Corinthians 12:4–12:

> "*Now there are diversities of gifts, but the same Spirit.
> And there are differences of administrations, but the same
> Lord. And there are diversities of operations, but it is the
> same God which worketh all in all. But the manifestation
> of the Spirit is **given to every man** to profit withal. **Or to
> one is given by the Spirit** the word of wisdom; to another
> the word of knowledge by the same Spirit; To another faith
> by the same Spirit; to another the gifts of healing by the
> same Spirit; To another the working of miracles; to another
> prophecy; to another discerning of spirits; to another divers
> kinds of tongues; to another the interpretation of tongues.
> But all these worketh that one and the selfsame Spirit,
> **dividing it to every man** severally as he will. For as the body
> is one, and hath many members, and all the members of
> that one body, being many, are one body: so also is Christ.*"
> (emphasis added)

This scripture tells us that the manifestations, or gifts of the
Spirit are given to men. They are from the Spirit, but the Spirit
expects us to work with the gifts. One of the gifts, the **working
of miracles**, is a good example of this. In verses twenty-nine and
thirty of 1 Corinthians 12, it says, "*Are all apostles? are all prophets?
are all teachers? are all **workers of miracles**? Have all the gifts of healing?*

do all speak with tongues? do all interpret?" (emphasis added). The answer is, "No!" These gifts are given only to certain people who are also given the ability to work with them. Paul used the word *"**workers**"* (verse 29). Jesus used this same verbiage when He sent the disciples out in Matthew 10:10: *"The **workman** is worthy of his meat [wages]"* (emphasis added). We are the workers; we are co-laborers with Christ. *"The harvest truly is plenteous, **but the labourers are few**"* (Matthew 9:37 emphasis added). We must stop being lazy, take responsibility, and stop expecting God to do everything for us. We must work and labor.

Understand your significance in what God is doing in the earth realm. You must understand that you are inseparable from God. Open your mind and receive the truth that you are of God, God dwells in you, you are His child, and you're not a mere man. We, as the body of Christ with a better covenant and better promises, need to grasp who we are in God. Refuse the Pharisee spirit that tries to ensnare you with false humility and false identity spirits, so you won't acknowledge your position and place in God.

Psalm 82:6 reads, *"I have said, **ye are gods**; and all of **you are children of the most High**."* [Emphasis added]. In this Old Testament Scripture, God gave us our identity in Him. Let's look at a New Testament Scripture. John 10:33–35 says:

> *"The Jews answered him, saying, For a good works we stone thee not; but for blasphemy; and **because that thou, being a man, makest thyself God.** Jesus answered them, **is it not written in your law, I said ye are gods? If he called them gods,** unto whom the word of God come, the **scripture cannot be broken.**"* [Emphasis added]

Jesus was saying to the Pharisees that if the law says we are gods then it cannot be broken.

The job of the Pharisee spirit is to get you to discredit your identity and position in God.

The Pharisees didn't want to kill Jesus because of His works. They wanted to kill Him for knowing and acknowledging His identity in God (John 10:33). Knowing who you are, and what you are "*ye are gods*" will enable you to walk in your full calling. When you realize your identity, you will be "*conformed to the image of His Son*" (Romans 8:29). Get ready for a new outlook on life as you break the false identity wall.

I would like to address one last false humility doctrine promoted to the public. This false identity spirit is called the "**nameless generation**" spirit. I have heard several famous pastors and preachers utter this unbiblical doctrine. It is false because it goes against one of the blessings of Abraham that we Gentile believers now have access to according to Galatians 3:14. That blessing is that "*he will make our name great*" (see Genesis 12:2). Jesus wants us to be seen and heard. He wants us to be, famous, and well known. He told us in Matthew 10:27: "*What I tell you in darkness, that speak ye in the light: and what ye hear in the ear, that preach ye upon the housetops.*" (emphasis added). The Lord doesn't want us to be shy quiet people. He wants us to shout His Gospel from the rooftops. I heard Jentezen Franklin say that the difference between a preacher and a teacher is, "one tells it, and one yells it." We must yell the good news. What is news? News simply means "to broadcast, advertise, promote, proclaim and network information from a certain source." If, we are not doing that, we are not fully spreading the good news of Jesus.

107

Let's keep the false identity/false humility doctrine from stealing our chance to build heaven on earth. Search the Scripture for yourself discover who you really are, and T.A.P!

—◊—

I pray in the name of Jesus that the invisible walls in your life will be torn down so that you can awaken to freedom in the Spirit of God and walk in your full calling. I pray that you find your identity in Christ and receive the full benefits of your inheritance in God. I pray that the social, racial, economic, and false identity walls will be broken and shattered forever. May the love of God over shadow your heart toward others in Jesus name.

Chapter 8

How to T.A.P.

Learn to Get Drunk

I'm not referring to alcoholic beverages or intoxicating liquor. In this segment, I'm addressing the new wine of the Spirit of God.

In the physical realm, wine is an alcoholic drink created from fermented grapes. In the spiritual realm, wine is the outpouring of God's anointing. Let's read a passage from the Scripture that describes wine: "*Neither do they put new wine into old wineskins, or else the wineskins break, the wine is spilled, and the wineskins are ruined. But they put new wine into new wineskins and both are preserved* " (Matthew 9:17, NKJV). One of the problems in the church is that they want new anointing poured into old vessels. This particular Scripture is an explanation about fasting (see verses 14–16), but it also outlines a strategy for looking at things differently. To get new wine, you have to get rid of your old ways, old traditions, and old methods. A 1930's message will not be effective in the new millennium. The modern day church aren't reaching the youth of America today. The reason being is that they are preaching an eight track tape message to an iPad generation. We must learn to become all things to all men, in order to win some for the Lord (1 Corinthians 9:22).

Oftentimes, when wine is involved, there is a party or celebration going on. We are so caught up with routine and religion that, we neglect our relationships with God and with people. As we read in Luke 2:52: "*Jesus increased in wisdom and stature, and in favor with God and man.*" An increase in the anointing brings favor with God and man. A lot of us know how to be good sons and daughters to God, but we are terrible brothers and sisters to one another. Jesus told us that people will know we are His, by the love we show to each other (John 13:35). We must learn how to get "drunk" together in the Spirit with kindness, compassion, and forgiveness (see Ephesians 4:32).

Many churches host revival meetings or conferences when they are spiritually dry. They say, "Come as you are!" Unfortunately, a majority of attendees leave the same way they came in. The only thing that is revived and renewed is the same watered down, lukewarm spirit. We need something beyond a revival. We need a restructuring. Today's revivalists are looking for God's Spirit to move the way He did in past revivals'. But, the Lord wants to do a new thing and pour out new wine.

Those with the Pharisee spirit love to hold on to the traditional way of doing things. They can't wrap their minds around God's new concepts. Anything that seems foreign to their protocol is written off as witchcraft, emotionalism, or just not "of God." The Bible says we are a peculiar people (1 Peter 2:9). I would rather look peculiar to man, than to be peculiar because of man.

Let's go to the winepress and learn how wine is created.

The winepress consisted of an area called the "treading floor." It was often cut from stone which included a drainage hole near the bottom, so that grape juices could flow into the collecting pool beneath the floor. Grapes were then placed on the treading floor where men used their feet to crush them. In Scripture, this process is often associated with the execution of God's wrath. Revelation 19:15 says: "*And out of his mouth goeth a sharp word, that with it **he should smite the nations**: and he shall rule them with a rod of iron: and he **treadeth the winepress** of the **fierceness and wrath of Almighty God**.*" (emphasis added). Everyone wants the new wine of God's Spirit, but they don't want the judgment and the spirit of repentance that comes with it.

In the winemaking process, you have to pick out the grapes, and then you have to stomp on them to press out the juice. The Holy Spirit is telling the church the same thing. First, you must get picked out, and then you must be picked on, stomped on, and trampled over. God is going to have to squeeze you until all the dross, dryness, and deadness of spirit is taken out of you. Another reason we can't receive new wine is that we haven't made proper use of the old wine yet. Some of us have received impartations that we haven't accessed or used. Most impartations come in seed form, so you must become a glory chaser in order to develop that particular anointing.

Some impartations do come fully formed. Once an imparta-tion is received, it's the job of the recipient to exercise the gift. Many people think exercising the gift means going out and minis-tering or laying hands on and prophesying over people. That's not the case. Exercising the gift involves building up and developing the anointing through fasting, praying, speaking in tongues, and worship. These principles send growth hormones to your spiritual baby (gift) to assist in full-term birthing.

How do we get the new wine or T.A.P.? Well, let's look at a scrip-tural pattern to help us out. John 2:3 reads, "*And **when they wanted wine**, the mother of Jesus said unto him, **They have no wine**" (emphasis added). First, we have to desire and be thirsty to get the new wine to come. Second, we must recognize that we have run out of wine. Many pastors, prophets, and evangelists are still active in ministry work, but they were fired a long time ago.

This is the only job that allows you to work after you've been laid off. People are not getting healed, saved, or set free because the minister is riding on a low tank of gas. He can't take the people far in the spirit because he is on "E." Fill up your tank before you offer anyone a ride in the spirit.

Let's look at the next step. John 2:5 reads, "*His mother saith unto the servants, Whatsoever he saith unto you, do it.*" I want to point out two key points here. Jesus mother spoke to the servants, to get the new wine, you need to have a servant's heart and mentality. Some of you might say, "I serve in my church and ministry." That may be true, But, do you serve without question and without your own motives or agendas? These servants followed the commands of Jesus mother without looking for recognition from Jesus. Mary, the mother of Jesus, was not even the servants' master at this wedding. But, because they had servants' hearts, they listened and responded to authority even when they did not have to.

Point two: Mary told the servants to do whatever Jesus told them to do. In today's society, individuals will adhere to their pastor's commands more than they adhere to God's commands. This also proves that Mary could not save the wedding or perform any miracles herself. She simply directed the servants to the one and only main source, Jesus. So, for those religions that encourages prayer towards Mary or any other saints to talk to God for them, just remember: Mary referred the people back to Jesus, not herself.

Jesus said, "*No man cometh unto the Father, but by me*" (John 14:6). Going further along in John 2, it tells us in verse six that "*there were set there six waterpots of stone, after the manner of the purifying of the Jews, containing two or three firkins apiece."* (emphasis added). Remember, the water was there for purification. We must purify ourselves before God can turn our water into new wine. We must be consecrated, sanctified, and live holy before the Lord. In 2 Timothy 2:21, we read, *"If a man therefore **purge himself** from these, he shall be a **vessel** unto **honour**, **sanctified**, and meet [useful] for the master's use, and prepared unto every good work"* (emphasis added).

The Lord wants to use us, but we must first be purged. The word purge means "to extract" or "to cleanse thoroughly." We must find every known and unknown sin and extract them by force. The body of Christ must force itself out of sin and into holiness. Compromising in the realm of sin isn't an option anymore.

Last but not least, John 2:7 says, *"Jesus saith unto them, **Fill the waterpots with water.** And they filled them up to the brim."* (emphasis added). Water signifies the Spirit. Jesus wanted the servants to fill these vessels up with water (the Spirit). We must learn to keep our vessels of our bodies filled with the Holy Ghost. Praying in tongues is one way to do this. Jude 1:20 says, *"But ye, beloved, building up yourselves on your most holy faith, praying in the Holy Ghost."* So let's get drunk in the Holy Ghost.

If you have not been baptized in the Holy Spirit, please repeat this prayer:

Jesus, I accept you as my Lord and Savior. I believe you died on a cross and rose from the dead. Come into my heart, and make me clean from all my sins. I renounce satan and every evil covenant I made with him by indulging in sin. Forgive me. I repent from my evil and disobedient ways. Now, Holy Spirit, I welcome you into my life. Baptize me with your Spirit and fire, and give me the evidence of speaking in tongues because your word said, "If ye then, being evil, know how to give good gifts unto your children: how much more shall your heavenly Father give the Holy Spirit to them that ask him?" (Luke 11:13). So we declare and decree that it is done in the mighty name of Jesus Christ!

T.A.P. through Mentorship

Mentorship is an intriguing part of the Christian walk. A mentor is a counselor who teaches and guides. A mentor deals with the mental, yes the mentality. Mentality means "a habit of the mind." A good mentor will help their subject reshape and redirect the habits of the mind. A mentor will mold and structure the right information or revelation to benefit that individual. Mentors help us to grow and become fruitful.

There is a doctrine that says we don't need to listen to man, only to God. This is true in one sense, but not true in another. Let's look at what the Bible says about this doctrine: "*And he gave some,* **apostles;** *and some,* **prophets;** *and some,* **evangelists;** *and some* **pastors** *and* **teachers;** *For the* **perfecting (equipping) of the saints,** *for the* **work of the ministry,** *for the* **edifying of the body** *of Christ*" (Ephesians 4:11–12, emphasis added). Many people misinterpret this Scripture. The fivefold ministry equips the saints for the work of ministry, the saints do not equip or perfect themselves. Some might say, "*The Holy Spirit teaches me all things*" (1 John 2:27). It is absolutely true that the Holy Spirit teaches us all things, but we must remember that He often does it through the fivefold ministry. If the Holy Spirit taught us all things only, well explain why you didn't receive certain revelations or information until a man spoke it to you through teaching or prophecy. If that's really the case, we can do away with churches, pastors, bible studies etc... we can just stay at home and let the Holy Spirit teach us everything.

The Holy Spirit is a gift that has been given to us, but the five-fold ministry is also a gift. Ephesians 4:7–8 says, "*Unto every one of us is given grace according to* **the measure of the gift of Christ**. *Wherefore he saith, When he [Jesus] ascended up on high, he led captivity captive, and* **gave gifts unto men**." You notice Paul says "gift**s**," plural. A few verses later, he lists those gifts: apostles, prophets, evangelists, pastors, and teachers. So, besides the infilling of the Holy Spirit, Jesus gives the body of Christ other humans on earth as tools to assist us in finishing the work of ministry, that He and His Father started. I would like to stress that when he said *"and gave gifts unto men"* that didn't mean men received gifts, but it actually meant, men where the gifts given to mankind from God. We are the gift!

Many people eliminate the importance of others from their Christian walk for several reasons. Some may have experienced bad relationships in their childhood or later on in life through an abusive marriage or friendship. Even worse, they may have encountered religious Pharisees in the church that left them with church hurt and distrust in their hearts. This person can be recognized by their insistence that someone is trying to control them. This statement is spoken out of fear of being hurt. Many people mistake order for control, and confidence for being cocky. The truth of the matter is God has given us rules and protocol to follow. This keeps the purpose of His Kingdom decent and in working order. We can find excuses, and even Scriptures, to justify why we should not trust man. At the end of the day, they don't stand up to a comprehensive study of the subject. Remember Jesus had to become a man to save mankind.

Some people don't trust others because they are concerned about encountering false prophets. Indeed, there are false prophets, but there are also real prophets. To have a false or fake version of something, you have to have a real one to copy, whether it's teeth or money or prophets. It's easy to detect false prophets; you don't have to be super spiritual or a rocket scientist to recognize them. Matthew 7:20 says, *"Wherefore by their fruits ye shall know them"* not by miracles, signs and wonders. So we don't judge them by signs they perform, but by fruit they bare. What fruits am I referring too? The fruits of the Spirit of course. You will find a great list of them in Galatians 5:22–23. If a prophet (or anyone claiming to be of the fivefold ministry) is not showing those fruits, then they are false. The fruit is based on the character of that individual not the gift of that person.

Matthew 7:21 reads, "*Not everyone that saith unto me, Lord, Lord, shall enter into the kingdom of heaven; but he that doeth the will of my Father which is in heaven.*" People sometimes say this verse speaks about false prophets. I don't think so. A false prophet is not someone who calls Jesus Lord or Savior. A false prophet comes in their own name, not in Jesus name. A false prophet does not acknowledge that Jesus came in the flesh. According to 1 John 4:2, "*Hereby know ye the Spirit of God: Every spirit that confesseth that Jesus Christ is come in the flesh is of God.*" So John shows us that a false prophet does not confess Jesus Christ as Lord or admit He came in the flesh.

I believe Matthew 7:21 is talking about fleshly believers. There is a difference between a fleshly prophet and a false one. Notice in Matthew 7:21 when Jesus says that "**not everyone**" who calls Him Lord will enter heaven. A false prophet can't call Jesus Lord because that would mean He is of God, and Jesus would be his Lord. When this Scripture says "*not everyone,*" it is referring to the average believer.

One day the Holy Spirit rebuked me, saying, "*Shawn, stop worrying about false prophets they are easy to spot.* He said "*Worry about false Christians.*" The ones who talk about everyone in the church, but crying at the alter every week, the ones who kiss up to the pastor, but talk behind his back, the ones who speak in tongues on Sunday, and curse people out at work on Monday, the ones who slander every prophet name, but not doing half of what that

116

prophet is doing for the Kingdom, the ones who are praising to the devil music in the club on Friday and Saturday night, but come sing worship in the choir on Sunday morning. Those who I just describe; are more dangerous then any false prophet that walks the earth. So stop being afraid of false prophets they are easy to spot, but really beware of the false carnal minded Christian they are the bigger threat.

Matthew 7:15–20 describes the false prophet, but Matthew 7:21–23 is about the disobedient Christian. Let's look at Matthew 7:22: "*Many will say to me in that day, **Lord, Lord,** have **we not prophesied** in thy name? And in thy name have **cast out devils**? And in thy name **done many wonderful works**?*" (emphasis added). Notice again Jesus speaks of "many," referring to average Christians. He then goes on to say what they would be doing, like prophesying, casting out devils, and performing many wonders. Some of you may say, "Well, psychics prophesy, and the Bible says the antichrist will do many false signs and lying wonders" (see 2 Thessalonians 2:9). That's all true, but remember they will perform false signs and lying wonders, not true signs and true wonders. That mean it will not last and it's a hoax, basically showcase magic and trickery, not manifestation of the spiritual world.

Here is one thing that satan and a false prophet can't do, and that's cast out demons.

Matthew 12:26 reads, "*And if Satan cast out Satan, he is divided against himself; how shall then his kingdom stand?*" This verse tells why satan and false prophets cannot cast out demons, especially in the name of Jesus. I state again that Matthew 7:22 is referring to the rebellious Christian, not the false prophet. People of God, I've said all this to say this: let's stop making excuses for why we cannot follow man's directions when it comes to the things of God. Learn to look at yourself and your own errors before you point fingers

117

and scream, "False prophet!" The Bible says to test the spirit by the Spirit. It does not say to test the man. Learn how to discern spirits and not judge people.

Now, I'd like to discuss the doctrine of multiple teachers. It's an epidemic in modern day society that must be stopped. I call it an "epidemic" because the word means "a break out that affects many individuals at the same time in a particular area." This particular epidemic is called *church hopping*. A church hopper is someone who hates being accountable to any kind of authority figure. Accountability brings credibility. The church hopper is a spiritual vampire who sucks the blood of Jesus out of each church they attend, leaving destruction, gossip, and disaster in their path.

We all know that anything with two heads is a monster. You can only have one spiritual head. "Why is that?" you ask. Look at Luke 16:13: "*No servant can serve two masters: for either **he will hate the one**, and **love the other**; or else **he will hold to the one**, and **despise the other**. Ye cannot serve God and mammon.*" (emphasis added). We know that Scripture is explaining the dangers of serving mammon. But this revelation also refers to earthly masters. You can't serve in one church, and then another, or serve in one ministry, and then another. That reflects on your character, and shows a lack of integrity because you're not faithful to your leader. Please don't misunderstand what I'm saying. I do believe in fellowshipping with other churches and other believers. But, I also believe that, if you have multiple teachers, it will create a conflict of interest. Ephesians 4:14 reads: "*That we henceforth **be no more children, tossed to and fro**, and **carried about with every wind of doctrine**, by the sleight of men, and cunning craftiness, whereby **they lie in wait to deceive**.*" [Emphasis added].

When you have more than one teacher, you are being tossed to and fro by different wind and doctrine. One church is feeding you steak, the next one is feeding you ice cream, and another one is feeding you pork. This causes spiritual constipation and confusion. You won't know what to believe. One teacher teaches the glory, another teaches repentance, and the other teaches grace. Now, you're confused about your doctrinal beliefs. The scriptures also states that deception happens. Where there is multiple doctrines deception follows.

In Scripture, you don't see God the Father, God the Son, and God the Holy Spirit teaching at the same time, even though they are all one. In John 16:7 *Jesus said, "Nevertheless I tell you the truth;* **It is expedient for you that I go away: for if I go not away**, *the Comforter* **will not come** *unto you;* **but if I depart, I will send him unto you.**" (emphasis added). Jesus was letting the disciples know that it was beneficial to them for Him to leave. If He didn't exit, the Holy Spirit, who was another teacher, could not enter. They couldn't have more than one teacher at a time.

Even John the Baptist told his disciples that he must decrease, and let Jesus increase (John 3:30). John knew that the people couldn't follow more than one doctrine. There are other biblical examples of mentoring relationships, such as Timothy following Paul. He did not follow Peter, James, John, or the other apostles. Paul was his only mentor. The disciples followed Jesus. Joshua followed Moses. Elisha followed Elijah only, 2 Kings 2 tells the story of how Elijah tried to leave Elisha three times: when he went to Bethel, Jericho, and then the Jordan. But the protégé, Elisha, said something powerful to Elijah every time: "*As the LORD liveth, and as thy soul liveth,* **I will never leave thee**" (2 Kings 2:2, 4, 6, emphasis added). This singular devotion was the key that led to Elisha receiving the double-portion anointing from Elijah.

Faithfulness is the key to the double-portion anointing. Elisha knew Elijah was going to be taken up, and so did the sons of the prophets, but Elijah wanted to test Elisha's faithfulness to serve him. Faithfulness is one of the fruits of the spirit found in Galatians 5:22. If the body of Christ learns how to stick with their leaders to the end, they can receive that leader's mantle. But, we are a microwave generation that wants to get hands laid on us today, then go do healing crusades tomorrow. It doesn't work like that. You must serve and be faithful to the leader and his ministry to receive what he has.

Some of you are saying, "Well, I don't need to wait on man. The Holy Spirit will anoint me." That is true, but remember Elisha asked for a double portion of Elijah's spirit not the Holy Spirit:

> *"And so it was, when they had crossed over, that Elijah said to Elisha, "Ask! What may I do for you, before I am taken away from you?" Elisha said, "Please let a **double portion of your spirit be upon me**." So he said, "You have asked a hard thing. Nevertheless, **if you see me when I am taken from you, it shall be so for you**; but if not, it shall not be so." (2 Kings 2:9–10, NKJV).*

Our individual spirit lives inside of us, along with the Holy Spirit. Elisha wanted the attributes and traits of his mentor. He desired Elijah's spirit. That was why, after Elijah was taken up, Elisha started performing miracles similar to those his teacher had performed during his earthly ministry. We all may have the Holy Spirit, but we all have different manifestations of His gifts. 1 Corinthians 12:40 tells us: "*Now there are **diversities of gifts**, but the same Spirit.*" So, yes, you may have some gifts, but not all. Every ministry has its own particular anointing. 1 Corinthians 14:32 tells us: *And the spirits of the prophets are subject to the prophets.* If your called to be a prophet, not only do you need the Holy Spirit, but also the spirit of the prophets. According to prophetic scripture John the Baptist had the spirit of Elijah read MalachI 4:5 and Luke 1:11-17.

We may have the spirit of prophecy and may prophesy, but that doesn't mean you have the spirit of the prophet, that allows you too walk in the office of the prophet. Trust me it's a big difference.

In a previous chapter, I mentioned that you have your majors and your minors.

One ministry's major might be healing while another's major might be prophecy or the working of miracles. Ministries that have similar majors will still yield diverse manifestations of those gifts. Some may experience heavy gold dust at their meetings, and others may experience instant weight loss in their meetings. Some may have many sick people healed at their services. Still yet, others will see manifestations of multiple gifts, or all of the gifts.

Whatever the case may be, if you are under the covering of a ministry, you will receive its particular anointing. Remember, the mantle is on the man, not the Holy Spirit. In 1 Corinthians 12:7 we read, "*But the manifestation of the Spirit is **given to every man** to profit withal*" (emphasis added). Even though the mantle comes from God, it's still assigned to a particular individual or ministry.

The following "**M**'s" of ministry will help you discern if you are following the right ministry. He must be a **m**an (1) with a **m**antle, (2) with a **m**essage, (3) with a **m**andate, (4) with a **m**anifestation, (5) with a **m**inistry that's (6) on a **m**ission, and who knows (7) how to **m**anage his **m**oney. If you don't see all of these qualifications in that one leading the ministry, then you're following the wrong leader.

Before I close this subject, I want to address one last vital point. To avoid being hurt, misused, or lied to, avoid this one mistake: Don't look for a church home or a mentor. Let them find you. Remember, Jesus picked His disciples. In John 15:16 Jesus said, "*Ye have not chosen me, but I have chosen you, and ordained you."* Paul picked Timothy (Acts 16:1–3). Elijah picked Elisha: *"So he [Elijah] departed thence, and **found Elisha** the son of Shaphat, **who was plowing** with twelve yoke of oxen before him, and he with the twelfth: and **Elijah** passed by him, and **cast his mantle upon him**"* (1 Kings 19:19, emphasis added).

Your mentor or pastor must find you "plowing." He must see if you are worthy of the anointing. Notice that Elijah cast the mantle on Elisha before he actually received it. I believe it was because he wanted to see if it fit Elisha. Some of us are trying to put on shoes and mantles that don't fit. I tell all my protégés, "You can ask me questions, but don't question me. Because if you know what you are doing, then you don't need me." That is like telling a mechanic who has been fixing cars for years how to fix your vehicle. We must practice the law of the student and learn to listen to authority. If we can grasp this principle and the importance of mentorship, then we can receive a double-portion anointing. So, open your heart to this principle and T.A.P.

Mountain Moving Faith

The following principle is probably one of the most important, because it is the access code to all the other principles. This method is needed to enter into or move in the glory. The principle I speak of is faith!

Let's begin by defining what faith is from worldly and scriptural perceptions. Webster's Dictionary defines faith as "allegiance or loyalty and duty to someone," "fidelity to a promise or trust," or "reliance." It also says that faith can be a belief and loyalty to God. It's the Scriptures of religious writings, or a system of religious beliefs. I don't know if Webster was a Christian or not, but he sure sounds like one. We find another definition of faith in Romans 3:3, which states, "*For what if some did not believe? Shall their unbelief make the faith of God without effect?*" This "faith" would be God's fidelity to a promise. But the majority of the time, it means trust and reliance.

The word faith occurs only twice in the Old Testament. There are other forms of the word, such as faithful or faithfulness, but they don't occur frequently. What we find in the Old Testament is not so much a doctrine of faith, but examples of it, such as Abraham having faith in God's promise to him. Abraham's faith is mentioned in Genesis 15:6 and is recounted in Galatians 3:6–9. Also, Hebrews 11 lists Old Testament figures that lived by faith, trusting in God's fidelity to His promises.

The New Testament speaks of faith several hundred times. The promised Messiah had finally come. The religious leaders and many others did not receive Him because He did not appear in the form that they envisioned. It required true faith to believe that Jesus of Nazareth was the promised Messiah. It was not long before the term "*to believe*" meant "to become a Christian." Thus the New Testament ranks faith high among human acts and experiences.

All throughout the Gospels, Jesus rebuked His disciples that lacked faith and rewarded those who had much faith. Doubt is the weed that chokes the seed of faith and hinders it from growing. Mark 11:23 gives us the recipe:

> *For verily I say unto you, That whosoever shall say unto this mountain, Be thou removed, and be thou cast into the sea; and **shall not doubt in his heart**, but shall believe that those things which he saith shall come to pass; he shall have whatsoever he saith. [Emphasis added.]*

We must remove doubt from our hearts so our faith can flourish. We need mountain moving faith. Doubt comes from unbelief. People can pray in agreement, but if there is a residue of doubt from the spirit of unbelief, then the prayer won't work. My definition of F.A.I.T.H. is Finding Away In Trusting Him. It's a trust issue. No healthy relationship can last without trust. Jesus is the husband; we are his bride. We must trust that our headship (Jesus) will love, provide for, protect, and care for us in all areas of our lives. The Hebrew word translated as "faith" is *emuwn*, which means "establish," "trusting," or "trustworthiness." The Lord is established, so why do we lack faith when we know deep down that He can, and already has, solved all our problems?

All we have to do is confess and allow His Spirit to flow.

In 2 Corinthians 13:1 we read: "*In the mouth of two or three witnesses shall every word be established.*" (emphasis added). Here, we see that faith comes from the confession realm. Romans 10:17 says, "*So then faith comes by hearing, and hearing by the word of God*" (NKJV). You can't hear unless you are speaking. Therefore you can't expect faith to come from the mere reading of the Word. You must speak the Word so you can hear it in your spirit. Reading is for the mind, but speaking is for the spirit. Jesus said, "*The words that I speak unto you, they are Spirit, and they are life*" (John 6:63, emphasis added). Once the Word of God is spoken from the spirit, it accesses faith, and faith breathes life into any situation.

Speaking God's Word is one facet of faith. If faith comes by hearing and hearing by the Word, then how can people who only have part of the Bible, or no Bible at all, have faith? Hebrews 11:1–2 states, "*Now faith is the substance of things hoped for, the evidence of things not seen. For by it the elders obtained a good report.*" Verses three through thirty-nine recount the stories of the elders of faith, such

as Abel, Enoch, Isaac, Jacob, Joseph, Abraham, Sarah, and Noah.
All of these elders had something in common: they didn't have
the *logos*, which is the written word. They had the *rhema* or audible word of God Himself, and that produced their faith. Faith
comes not only by hearing the written Word, but also by hearing
the *rhema*, or audible voice of God, through a prophetic utterance
in your spirit. We need both the *logos* and the *rhema* to build our
faith.

Jude 20 says, "*Building up yourselves on your most holy faith, praying
in the Holy Ghost.*" This Scripture shows us that faith comes, and is
established, through praying in the Spirit. This verse lets us know
that faith came by the *rhema (spirit)* word of God, not just the *logos*
of the written word. In this Scripture, and the majority of other
New Testament verses, "faith" is translated from the Greek word
pistis, which means "truth," "assurance," "belief," "faith," or "fidelity." In one instance the Greek word *elpis*, is translated as "faith"
(Hebrews 10:23). *Elpis* is usually translated as "hope," meaning
"expectation," "confidence," or "to anticipate with pleasure." The
word "Pleasure" means a feeling of satisfaction or enjoyment, or
a source of delight or joy. Your faith must be pleasurable. Instead
of walking in uncertainty, you must take pleasure in trusting God.
When there is no pleasure in faith, discouragement settles in, and
then the seed of doubt starts to grow. 'Enjoyment and pleasure
makes the delay process easier.

Proverbs 13:12 tells us, "*Hope deferred maketh the heart sick: but
when the desire cometh, it is a tree of life.*" "Hope" is translated from
the Hebrew word, *towcheleth,* meaning "expectation." The waiting
process of faith can be a burden to the flesh, but enjoyment comes
as we push through the trial. James 1:3–4 says, "*Knowing this, that
the **trying of your faith**, worketh **patience**. But let **patience** have her perfect work, that ye may be **perfect** and **entire, wanting nothing**"* (emphasis
added). Your faith must be tested and tried. A faith that is not

tested is a faith that can't be trusted. The trying of your faith produces maturity. Once faith is tested, patience starts to develop and grow.

Patience is one of the nine fruits of the Spirit (Galatians 5:22), and it is one of the most important fruits. Without patience, you can't love correctly. When your patience is short, you are not kind, or gentle. You don't have self-control when you're impatient. Peace is calmness, but when you don't have patience, you can't keep calm.

James 1:4 tells us, "*Let patience have her perfect work, that **ye may be perfect** and **entire, wanting nothing**"* (emphasis added). "Entire" means "having no part left out," "whole," or "complete." So, if it is through the working of patience that we'll be made perfect and whole, it must be one of the most important fruits of the Spirit. It is the fruit that builds faith. Once patience has done its job, there won't be anything lacking.

Galatians 6:9 conveys this same idea: "*Let us **not grow weary** in well doing: for in due season we shall reap, **if we faint not**"* (emphasis added). When we grow weary in our faith, it's because we lack patience. That lack of patience hinders our harvest. The Scripture says you will reap, if you don't grow weary. When you are weary that means your impatient. I'm telling you to not lose your patience! When you lose your patience, you lose your blessings. Through developing your patience, you will obtain great faith. Have patience so you may grow in your faith and lack nothing. T.A.P.!

Confession Brings Possession

What is a confession? "***Confess***" or "***confession***" in the New Testament is translated from the Greek word ***homologeo***, which means "to acknowledge or agree." Confession is the source of the power of agreement. "Agreement" is translated from two powerful words in Hebrew. One is *chozeh*, which means "beholder of vision." When you have the principle of confession and the power of agreement, you behold the vision of God. The second Hebrew word is *chazuwth*, which means "revelation" or "a compact agreement." Wow! That is powerful. This is why the enemy loves to cause disagreements. He works hard to bring dissension between children and parents, husbands and wives, employers and employees, neighbors and friends, pastors and church members, or one of his favorites, churches against churches. The list goes on and on. Why does he do this? He does not want Matthew 18:19 to come to pass: "*Again I say unto you, That **if two of you shall agree** [confess] on earth as touching anything that they shall ask, **it shall be done for them** of my Father which is in heaven.*" (emphasis added)

Whether it is you in agreement with God's Word, or you and another believer in agreement through prayer, confessions must be made with two or more parties involved. In Matthew 18:20 Jesus says, "*For where **two or three are gathered together** in my name, there am I in the midst of them*" (emphasis added). There are a lot of people who aren't in agreement, even though they are gathered together. This fosters disunity, which suppresses the anointing and prevents revelation from flowing.

Act 2:1 tells us, "*And when the day of Pentecost was fully come, they were all with one accord in one place.*" This coincides with Matthew 18:20, which says, "*Two or three are gathered together in my name [in one accord], there I am in the midst of them.*" Jesus knew mankind would have a problem getting on one accord because of their different opinions and doctrines. He knew they needed the triune God to give them the power of agreement. The significance and results of being "with one accord" (Acts 2:1) is clearly shown in the next verse: "*And suddenly there came a sound from heaven as of a rushing mighty wind, and it filled all the house where they were sitting"* (Acts 2:2). Heaven comes down when we are in unity.

Jesus knew mankind needed help finding divine unity. So, He set up a system to where He would show up when the people came together, on one accord, in His name. In Matthew 18:15-17 Jesus speaks on how to deal with someone who has committed an offense against another. In verse sixteen He says, *"But if he will not hear thee, then **take with thee one or two more**, that in **the mouth of two or three witnesses every word may be established**."* [Emphasis added]. This Scripture shows that the verbal confession of two or three people is powerful enough to establish God's word. I hope you caught that. The word was "established" through the mouths of the witnesses, not so much the hearts of the witnesses.

Sometimes the heart has to catch up with the mouth. The Word says, *"Out the abundance of the heart the mouth speaks"* (Matthew 12:34, NKJV). Jesus also says, in John 6:63, *"**It is the spirit that quickeneth**; the flesh profiteth nothing: the **words that I speak unto you**, they are **spirit**, and they are **life**."* (emphasis added). Jesus was saying that, even if you are speaking from your wicked, fleshly heart, confessing His words will quicken your spirit man, change your fleshly mindset, and bring you life more abundantly. It is not your words, but His words that are the spirit and life. The more you confess God's Word, the more it will quicken your spirit and bring life to your dead situation.

In Jeremiah 1:12 we read, *"Then said the LORD unto me, Thou hast well seen: for **I will hasten (watch) my word to perform it**."*(emphasis added). God's Word is meant to affect the earth realm. His Word is alive, and it displays action. Let's go to Ephesians 3:20, a frequently misunderstood Scripture. Verse twenty reads: *"Now unto him that is able to do exceedingly abundantly above all that we **ask** or **think**, according to the power that worketh in us"* (emphasis added). People think the "*power that worketh in us*" is the Holy Spirit. But, ask yourself how many people you know who have the infilling of the Spirit and yet, they don't operate in power. Let's take that thought to Proverbs 18:21: "*Death and life are in the **power of the tongue***" (emphasis added). Could it be that the "**power**" in Ephesians 3:20 refers to the "**asking**" realm of the tongue? God knows we don't know how to ask properly.

Romans 8:26 tells us, "*Likewise the **Spirit also helpeth our infirmities**: for **we know not what we should pray for** as we ought: but the Spirit himself maketh intercession [**confession**] for us with groanings which cannot be uttered.*" (emphasis added). The asking realm gives us access to the abundant lifestyle. Ignoring this principle has hindered the body of Christ from receiving their full inheritance. We have not because we ask not (see James 4:2). The Lord also knows man doesn't understand the abundant life. He says in John 10:10, "*I have come that they may have life, and that they may have it more abundantly*" (NKJV). How could He do that? Through His words, of course, because His words are spirit and life, abundant life! But, we have a part in this. We must activate it through the power that works in us. We must, use our tongues to ask. A confession a day keeps the devil away. The power that works in us is the power of our tongue.

The other missing ingredient in the confession principle is the thinking realm. Many people have the "name it and claim it" doctrine down to a science. The issue with many who practice this principle and see very little results, is that, they have the asking realm, but not the mentality to go with it. That's why some see results in the so called prosperity gospel while others still lack. Both parties may sow their seeds, and both may name and claim their harvests. However, one of them thinks like a rich man while the other still struggles with the doctrine of "God wants us rich and wealthy."

Let me give you an example. Matthew 6:4,6,18 says: **when you give**, **when you pray**, and **when you fast** in secret, God will reward you openly. In these passages, Jesus was giving us Kingdom principles to obtain God's rewards. Then there is the famous verse in Matthew 6:33 which states, "*But **seek ye first the kingdom of God**, and his righteousness; and **all these things shall be added** unto you*" (emphasis added). To gain access to God's blessings, you must seek the King and His Kingdom in order to gain access to God's blessings. The Kingdom is not the King. The Kingdom is the assets, domain, and principles of the King. Like I said in earlier chapters, you can find the prince in his principles. The principles are the characteristics of the Prince, it's the mentality and attitude of that individual. I also believe evil principalities are in peoples personalities. That's why many of us can't discern the demonic, because we preconceive that this is just that persons character. Not knowing, demons camouflage themselves through our free will. Before we can begin the work of Matthew 6:1–18, which is giving, praying, and fasting, these principle needs to be administered first.

Let's look at the chapter prior to that. Matthew 5:3–12 is referred to as "The Beatitudes." Before we can work a principle for an expected result, we must cultivate the proper attitude and mindset. Remember, Matthew chapters five and six go together because both were a part of the sermon on the mount. For example, "*Blessed are the meek: for they shall inherit the earth.*" There you have it, that's the formula. Jesus was saying if we have an attitude of meekness, we shall inherit earthly possessions. In this verse you find the attitude of the prince and the rewards for working His principle. As you confess, you must possess an attitude and mindset that coincides with the desired request. Let your mind line up with the vision, and God will send provision. T.A.P.!

Hands On Training

The following principle has been misunderstood and misused. It has diminished over the years because of a new doctrine concerning the glory of God. The principle I speak of is the "laying on of hands." "Hand" in Scripture is commonly used and is usually translated from the Hebrew word *yad* which means power.

Hands have literal uses but also are spoken of in figurative senses.

In Genesis 9:2 it infers strength or power: "*And the fear of you and the dread of you shall be upon every beast of the earth, and upon every fowl of the air, upon all that moveth upon the earth, and upon all the fishes of the sea; **into your hand are they delivered**.*" Deliverance lays in the power of the hand, whether it is God's hand or a human's hand. Genesis 48:14 illustrates another use of hands: "*And Israel stretched out his right **hand**, and laid it upon Ephraim's head, who was the younger, and his left **hand** upon Manasseh's head, guiding his **hands** wittingly; for Manasseh was the firstborn*" (emphasis added). This laying on of the hands signifies blessings and ordination. Without the laying on of the hands in the Old and New Testaments, one was not officially anointed or appointed for the position, office, or gifting that was passed on from the eldership. We find a clear example of this in 1 Timothy 4:14: "*Neglect not the **gift that is in thee**, which was **given thee by prophecy, with the laying on of the hands** of the eldership*" (emphasis added). A gift of the Spirit was given by physical contact through the laying on of hands.

In this verse, the gift was also given through prophecy. You can prophecy over someone, but without the laying on of hands, the ceremony, ordination, or gifting, is not complete. We also see this in Acts 13:2–3: "*As they ministered to the Lord, and fasted, the Holy*

*Ghost said, Separate me Barnabas and Saul for the **work whereunto I have called them**. And when they had **fasted** and **prayed, and laid their hands** on them, they sent them away"* (emphasis added).

Saul and Barnabas didn't become great apostles of the faith until prayer, fasting, and the laying on of hands was administered to them. The Holy Spirit spoke the calling, but man commissioned them through the laying on of hands. I see many women and men of God who have walked away from this practice. There are ministers who are convinced that worship and the atmosphere of glory will cause miracles to take place. This is true, but, I have observed many who came to a meeting for healing and left the meetings still diseased, blind, in wheelchairs, and not delivered. These ministers say it's up to the Lord to heal, or that the atmosphere of worship wasn't right.

When Jesus walked the earth, He did not have a worship service before He administered healing. He often laid hands on people. Matthew 17:16–17 tells us of a father crying out to Jesus to deliver his son: *"And I brought him to the disciples, and they could not cure him. Then Jesus answered and said, O faithless and perverse generation, how long shall I be with you? How long shall I suffer you? Bring him here to me."* If Jesus rebuked the disciples for not being able to cast out devils during His earthly ministry, I wonder what He thinks of the church today. When someone doesn't get healed, we often shift the blame to God. But it's God's will for everyone to be healed, set free, and delivered. We, as Christians, must start owning up to the part we play in the deliverance, healing, and wholeness of the people. If we took more time to minister to people through the laying on of hands, we would see more healings take place. Jesus gave us a good example in Luke 4:40: *"Now when the sun was setting, all they that had any sick with diverse diseases brought them unto him; and **he laid his hands on every one of them**, and healed them"* (emphasis added).

132

We often use the excuse that we can't lay hands on everybody, especially when we have large crowds. But, Jesus did it. Some estimate that the crowd spoken of in Luke 4:40 was several thousand people strong. I understand that circumstances sometimes prevent us from laying hands on everyone. But if we have the opportunity, we should lay hands on those who are really in need of prayer.

I am going to discuss several misunderstood or misinterpreted Scriptures concerning the reasons why we should not lay hands on people. The most famous one is 1 Timothy 5:22: "*Lay hands suddenly on no man, neither be partaker of other men's sins: keep thyself pure.*" Many think this Scripture means that we should not be quick to lay hands on anyone, which is true. But in context, it means not to be quick to commission anyone, especially those who are in sin. This does not refer to those who need healing administered to them. Jesus did not lay hands on everyone either, some only received their healing through their relentless faith (see Matthew 15:22-28). But for the most part he laid hands on thousands of people.

Another misunderstood Scripture is Acts 4:29–30, which is part of a prayer by the disciples: "*And now, Lord, behold their threatenings: and **grant unto thine servants**, that with all boldness they may speak thy word, By stretching forth **thine hand** to heal; and **that signs and wonders may be done by the name** of thy holy child Jesus.*" (emphasis added). We see in this verse that the Lord used His hands to do things. But this wasn't indicating that the Lord alone was going to perform miracles. The verse states that the signs and wonders would be done by the name of Jesus, not by His hands. The miracles are done by Jesus name but through the disciples' hands. See, the Lord works *with* us, not *for* us. When the Lord stretch forth His hands it's usually through your hands, because His work is finished.

I mentioned Mark 16:18 in a previous chapter: "*They shall take up serpents; and if they drink any deadly thing, it shall not hurt them;*

they shall lay hands on the sick and they shall recover" (emphasis added). This clearly states that we will be the ones laying hands, not Him. Jesus would not contradict Himself. This was the last statement Jesus made before His ascension. His physical work was finished. Further along in the chapter, Mark 16:20 tells us what followed: "*And they went forth, and preached everywhere, the Lord **working with them**, and **confirming the word with signs following**. Amen*" (emphasis added). Again, the Lord worked ***with*** them, not ***for*** them.

The Lord's job is to confirm the word with a sign. It's our job to preach the word and lay hands. John 14:12 tells us, "*Verily, verily, I say unto you, He that believeth in me, **the works that I do shall he do also; and greater works than these shall he do**; because **I go unto my Father**"* (emphasis added). It is Jesus job to go to the Father, and it's our job to do the work.

What is the work? There is a list in Matthew 10:8: "*Heal the sick, cleanse the lepers, raise the dead, cast out devils: freely ye have received, **freely give**.*" Don't charge anyone for the gift you receive from God through the laying on of hands. This is a serious point. In Acts 8:17–18 we read that the apostles "*Then **laid they their hands** on them, and they received the Holy Ghost. And when Simon saw **that through laying on of the apostles hands** the **Holy ghost was given**, he offered them money*" (emphasis added).

It was through the laying on of hands of the apostles, that the Holy Spirit was given and the people received the gift of tongues. Simon the sorcerer realized this and wrongly desired to buy God's freely given gift. Jesus told His disciples to remember, "*Freely ye have received, freely give*" (Matthew 10:8). Simon wanted to buy the gift from the disciple's: "saying, *Give me also this **power** that on whomsoever **I lay hands**, he may receive the Holy Ghost*" (Acts 8:19, emphasis added).

Simon the sorcerer even caught the revelation that the power was administered through the laying on of the apostle's hands. If a sorcerer can grasp this principle why can't we? Think about it. In a lot of churches, many people get born again but never receive the Holy Spirit. If they do, it's often later on from another ministry or an invited evangelist. Perhaps it's because we have altar calls without laying on hands for the baptism. These days, people have adapted to allowing the sovereign atmosphere of the glory realm to do everything for them. Jesus said the power is in the hand, so why don't we use this point of contact for healing, miracles, signs, and wonders?

As I indicated before, the Hebrew word **yad**, which is most often translated as "hand," indicates strength or power. Let's go back to Acts 4:30, which says, *"By stretching forth thine hands to heal; and that signs and wonders may be done by the name of thy holy child Jesus."* The first church wasn't asking God to come and do the work for them. They were asking Jesus to increase in their life, so they could heal the sick and perform signs and wonders boldly in Jesus name. To understand this theory, you must first understand what God's hand does: *"Thy right hand, O LORD, is become glorious in power: thy right hand, O LORD, hath dashed in pieces the enemy"* (Exodus 15:6). We see here that God's right hand is where His power lies. Luke 22:69 confirms this: *"Hereafter shall the Son of man sit on the right hand of the power of God."* The right hand of God is His power source, and the Son of man sits on that side. Who is that Son of man? Jesus, of course. In Acts 4:30 they were not asking Jesus to come back on the earth and show them how to administer healing again. They were asking the Father to give them more of the power of His Son, so they could do exploits like He did.

I am not saying the Lord doesn't heal without the laying on of hands. We have seen many miracles, healings, and deliverances without touching a single person. But, we have also seen many not healed because the minister refused to lay hands. If someone doesn't get healed, they say it wasn't God's timing or blame it on the atmosphere of glory not being strong enough or that persons faith. When you look at Mark 6:5–6, NIV even Jesus had to apply this principle when the atmosphere wasn't conducive. It reads: "*He [Jesus] could **not do any miracles there**, except **he lay his hands** on a few sick people and **heal them**. He was amazed at their lack of faith*" (emphasis added).

Jesus knew their faith wasn't there to receive sovereign miracles, but he didn't refuse the people their healing because he refused to lay hands. He kicked into gear two and started administering the glory through the point of contact with His hands. Many believe it's the anointing and not the glory when hands are laid. This is not true. The laying on of hands is just another way to minister in the glory. The reason many people get tired when they administer the glory through the laying on of hands, it's because they are ministering through the flesh, not the spirit. The laying on of hands has received a bad rep due to this.

I have ministered under the glory, with the laying on of hands, to hundreds and even thousands of people in one night without getting tired. To put this in perspective, we realize that we must ask the Lord to stretch His hands out to enforce His power on our enemies. We also know that allowing the Lord sovereign healing is always best. However, I want us to look inside ourselves and see if we are doing our part, as well. A time might come when we cannot wait until a band or worship leader sings the right songs to do miracles.

The Holy Spirit does not minister the glory the same way all the time. One day, He might tell you to lay hands, then the next day He might say, "Just proclaim the spoken word." No one has a patent on the Holy Spirit. Even Jesus did not minister the same way all the time. Remember, "*But all these worketh that one and self-same Spirit, dividing to every man **as he will**"* (emphasis added). Not as you will. We must get out of our routine and get back to the basic simplicity of the gospel, no matter how much revelation we get about the glory realm. We can never take away Jesus methods and commandments for how we should administer miracles as believers. See Mark 16: 15–18 and T.A.P.

This section wasn't intended to insult or undermine anyone who doesn't lay hands. It is meant to encourage us to go back to the days of our first love, before we learned about the glory, the days when we oiled everything we saw and were willing to even lay hands on our pets. This section was also not meant to give man praise. It is meant to help us recognize the role we play in the gifts of the Spirit being released. The Lord cannot break the jurisdiction He gave us. Jurisdiction means "the lawful right or power to interpret and apply the law of the territory within which that power is exercised." God gave us dominion in this jurisdiction (Genesis 1:26–28). He had to become man to save man. The job is up to us.

Let's end with a parable: Three little boys went into a store. The kind owner told them to get as much candy out of the candy jar as their hands could hold. Two of the boys stuck their hands in the jar, and each grabbed a handful. But, the third little boy just stood there. The owner told him again to grab a handful of candy from the jar. The little boy continued to stand there. So, the owner stuck his hand in the jar, pulled out the candy, and gave it to the little boy. Later, the other boys asked him why he had just stood there. He responded, I waited for the owner to do it because his hands were bigger than mine. When he stuck his hand in the jar, I got a lot more than if it were just my hand.

This parable is prophetic. Yes the Lord hands are bigger to get more done then if it was just in our hands. However, it's always for the purpose of taking what he has in His hands and place it in ours. That's what I call "hands on training." T.A.P.!

T.A.P. Through TV

I love watching Christian television. I was a new believer with a supernatural assignment, I needed a mentor in the supernatural. It was rare to find people in my city who moved in the glory. A lot of churches had the anointing, but they didn't have the revelation about the glory realm. When I showed up talking about seeing manifestations of gold dust, they thought I had gone off the deep end. So I watched Christian television networks and the Internet to learn more about the glory.

The show *It's Supernatural! with Sid Roth* caught my attention above the rest of the programs. I watched the show and saw average people moving in the glory and making it sound and look easy to do. I became a believing and faithful fan, watching the show every time it aired. Then, I went on the Internet and watched the archives. One day, I watched Pastor Tony Kemp on the show. He said he had watched archived shows just like me. He then had the chance to meet someone from the show who gave him in-depth mentoring about the glory. Before he knew it, he was on the show talking about his own encounters in the glory. I said to myself, "I am going to do the same thing that guy did."

Months passed, and my friend told me he'd had a dream that Sid Roth came to him and said, "Shawn has a book he needs to write about the supernatural." When he told me about the dream, I was excited, but I brushed it off because I didn't know the first thing about writing a book. I could barely read, so I knew it was just another pipe dream. Two years passed, and my ministry started to progress. I started running into people at conferences who were former guests on *It's Supernatural! with Sid Roth.*

One day, I was at a meeting in Dallas with David Herzog, and the Holy Spirit said, "*T.A.P. The Anointed Principles.*" Electricity went through my body. He said, "This is the book I want you to write. Start now!" My friend Joel, was with me for that encounter. The Lord reminded us of the dream he'd had two years prior.

Then, I met Kathie Walters. She walked up to me, touched me with her right index finger, and said, "Oh, a prophet!" I was almost knocked back. The people behind me felt the power. She told me, "If I touch you with my left hand, it means you'll just walk in the gift. But if I touch you with my right hand, you'll walk in that office." Then, she rebuked me for having a religious spirit. I took it with love. She is such a precious lady.

Mahesh Chavda prophesied over my wife and I concerning our ministry and my book. He also talked about how powerful our ministry would be, and said he wanted the first copy of my book when it was finished. Leif Heifland prophesied over me about the nations I would journey to. John Kilpatrick prophesied over me and said, "When you preach, you will have fire in your heart and tears in your eyes." Glenda Jackson and I are working together to open up the wells of revival. Joan Hunter and I became good friends. She is an awesome woman of God I was ordained under her minstry. Tony Kemp and I finally met. It was like history repeating itself. He agreed to be a spiritual mentor to me. Last but not least, I met Kevin Basconi, who gave me wisdom about writing and publishing the book. I love you guys, and thank you for helping me to T.A.P.!

Don't T.A.P. Out!

Hopefully, you have learned the "do's" of how to T.A.P. Now I will share the don'ts, or what you should not do once you have T.A.P.ed. I will point out a few hindrances that keep us from entering, or staying in, God's presence. There are a few questions I will answer: Why is staying in the presence of God is so important? Don't we have to have a life outside of God? If we are too heavenly minded, are we no earthly good? To answer the last question first, quite frankly, I would rather be heaven bound and no earthly good any day of the week.

Dwelling in God's presence is vitally important to your Christian walk, and here's why:

Job 2:7 says, "**So went Satan forth from the presence of the Lord and smote Job with sore boils from the sole of his foot unto his crown**" (emphasis added). The Lord had just given Job over to satan's hand, but He prohibited him from killing Job. Notice that satan didn't strike Job with boils until after he had departed from the presence of God. As long as you stay in God's presence, the enemy can't affect you. He must wait until you are not under the shadow of the Almighty (Psalm 91:1). Sickness, poverty, or demonic attack cannot penetrate your life as long as you're in God's presence.

Psalm 16:11 clearly states, "*Thou wilt show me the path of life: in thy presence is fullness of joy; at thy right hand there are pleasures for evermore*" (emphasis added). If you don't have fullness of joy, then you aren't in God's presence. If you are sick, or if your relationships is going sour, these are indications that there is a lack, or shortage, of God's presence in your life. We must strive for His presence like Moses did: "*And he [God] said, **My presence shall go with thee**, and I will give thee rest. And he [Moses] said unto him; If thy **presence go not with me**, carry us not up hence*" (Exodus 33:14–15 emphasis added).

140

This scripture indicates that, without God's presence, there is no physical, mental, or spiritual rest. Moses also informed the Lord that if His presence weren't there, he didn't want to go any farther on his journey. A lot of us are on a journey, but the Lord's presence isn't with us. We see it in churches where the buildings are being enlarged, even as the anointing is decreasing. It's about quality of spirit not about the quantity of people you can accumulate in your church.

Many churches, ministries, and synagogues around the world emphasize doctrine, theological studies, and belief systems. But very few of these teaches, and demonstrates the practice of entering into the presence of God. This principle is key in the daily maintenance of our Christian lifestyle. Let's get back to the basics.

No Greasy Grace

Grace is a touchy subject that most Christians do not like to debate. I believe grace is the power not to sin, not a license to sin. Jesus did not preach grace. He just demonstrated mercy to the people. Many get God's grace and God's mercy mixed up.

One definition of grace is an extension of time granted after a set date, such as for paying a debt. Jesus paid our debt through His death and gave us an extension of time to renew our fellowship with God the Father through accepting Him as our Savior. But, what did Jesus save us from? He saved us from sin. Jesus did not save us from hell. He saved us from the sin that leads us to hell. God had mercy on mankind and sent His Son to give us grace.

When you mention the removal of sin, or obeying God's commandments in the church, the first thing a person operating in excessive false grace doctrine would say is that you're operating in legalism. That person is under the spirit of compromise. Even the apostle of grace (Paul) mentions in Romans 7:12: "*Wherefore **the law is holy**, and **commandments holy**, and **just**, and **good**.*"(emphasis added). This is a New Testament Scripture that shows that law and commandments of the old covenant are flawless, and holiness is attached to them. Another Scripture the Apostle of grace mentions in Romans 7:14: "*For we know that **the law is spiritual**: but I am carnal, sold under sin.*"(emphasis added). It says the law is spiritual, but we are carnal, not the law. This is another Scripture that shows the good attributes of the law in the New Testament.

Then you go further down in that passage, and Paul makes a statement that sounds like a contradiction to his grace doctrine. In Romans 7:25 he says: "*I thank God through Jesus Christ our Lord. So then with **the mind I myself serve the law of God**; but **with the flesh the law of sin***" (emphasis added). This verse shows us that there are two different laws Paul is referring to. He says with his mind that he wants to serve the law of God, which is the Old Testament law.

There was no New Testament in Paul's day. There was only one testament, which was the Torah. The second law he mentions was the law of sin, or sin and death. Jesus saved us from the curse of the law (Galatians 5:13–14); he did not save us from obeying the law. That would be going against His Father rules. Any kid knows you do not disobey your parents rules, and don't expect to reap consequences. Paul said in Romans 7:7, "*What shall we say then? **Is the law sin? God forbid.** Nay, **I had not known sin, but by the law**: for **I had not known lust, except the law had said**, Thou shall not covet.*" (emphasis added).

In America, a lot of converts get saved, through the grace message, which is good. But 80 percent still continue in sin through filthy language, fornication, adultery, and all kinds of known sin. The first thing that comes out of their mouths is, "You can't judge me", if you decide to correct them on these issues. This non sense is caused because no one stresses, that it is not right in the sight of God. This is the reason we have homosexuals leading our worship teams, legal gay marriages, children out wedlock, kids in gangs and on drugs, while the pastors sit around doing nothing to correct the problem. Either they don't want to lose members, or they are too afraid to offend the flesh.

The preaching of the cross and remission of sins is, offensive to those who are perishing in sin (see 1 Corinthians 1:18). We must show these people where their particular transgressions are outlined in the Bible (the law). Salvation comes, only through grace by faith, not through the law. However as grace is for salvation, God's word (law) is for sanctification.

- *Psalm 119:153–154 says: "Consider mine affliction, and **deliver me:** for I do **not forget thy law**. Plead my cause, and **deliver me: quicken me according to thy word**" (emphasis added). It's through God's word (the law) that deliverance and quickening, or revival of the spirit takes place. You say, "Prophet, that's Old Testament." Well, let's look at what Jesus said. John 15:10 states, "If **ye keep my commandments, ye shall abide in my love**; even as **I** (Jesus) **have kept my Father's commandments** (the law), and **abide in his love**" (emphasis added). This shows us that Jesus himself obeyed God's law.*

People in the excessive false grace movement love to emphasize the Father's love over obeying His commandments. However, if there isn't true obedience, then there isn't true love. We may be in love with God, but we are not abiding in His love. To abide means "to remain; to conform; to comply with." When we are not obedient to God's commandments (the law), we are not in compliance with His love. The word comply means "to agree," "to consent to," or "to obey a command or wish." This definition says "obey a command." So, if we are not obeying God's principles, whether we are under grace or not, we can't claim to have the true love of God.

The message of excessive false grace has plagued the body of Christ. It has crippled the saints and caused many of them to compromise in their walk. They have given up on pressing towards the high mark. Isaiah 26:10 says, "*Let **grace be shown** to the wicked, yet will **he not learn righteousness**: in the land of uprightness will he deal unjustly, and **will not behold** the **majesty** of the Lord.*" (emphasis added). Grace does not teach us righteousness, it teaches us the mercy of God. During his earthly ministry, Jesus preached repentance and the Kingdom of God, but he never preached grace; he just showed mercy. Many believers want to see revival, but they don't want to hear the message that comes with it. We can't receive the manifestation without the message. What's the message? The message Jesus preached to the church and the world during His earthly ministry. The same message he expects us New Testament believers to preach. : "*repent for the Kingdom of Heaven is at hand*" (Matthew 4:17). Jesus made statements like, "*I am not come to call the righteous, but sinners to repentance*" (see Matthew 9:13).

If that's what Jesus was called to do, why are we missing it? The church has it backward. We preach grace to the church congregation and repentance to people outside the walls, when we are supposed to preach grace to the sinners, who don't know better, and repentance to the church, because we know the truth. Jesus exemplified this when he rebuked the Pharisees (church) of His days.

The repentance doctrine has been demonized in modern day Christianity as a form of legalism and condemnation. Romans 8:1 states, "*There is therefore **no condemnation** to them which are in **Christ Jesus**, who **walk not after the flesh**, but after the Spirit.*" (emphasis added).

144

If someone mentions repentance, and you feel condemned, then you're a fleshly believer. If a minister delivers a rebuke, and you get offended over his mention of the law, then you're in the flesh. If you feel offended and condemned, it's because the flesh doesn't want to die.

The Scripture says in Psalm 119:165: "*Great **peace have they which love thy law: and nothing shall offend them***" (emphasis added). When you love God's law, you shall have peace. Also, you won't be offended when the law is mentioned. If Paul's message of grace confuses you, study what Jesus preached and lived. In Matthew 8:4 Jesus said to a man after he healed him, "*But go thy way, **shew thyself to the priest**, and **offer the gift that Moses commanded**, for a testimony unto them.*" Jesus told the man to obey the law of Moses, because the law of Moses is His Father's word. Jesus didn't come to contradict His Father's word, he came to bring life to it (see Romans 7:6). In Matthew 5:17, Jesus said, "*Think **not that I am come to destroy the law**, or the prophets: **I am not come to destroy**, but to **fulfill**''* (emphasis added). Jesus emphasized that He came to fulfill the law, not to destroy or do away with it.

No one on earth is spotless enough to fulfill the whole law as Jesus did. Neither were the saints who have gone on to Heaven. He died so that, by His grace, we could fulfill the law as well. "*That the righteousness of the law might be fulfilled in us*" (Romans 8:4). God wants to fulfill the righteousness of the law in us and remove the curse of the law from us.

As much as, I love Paul's epistles and the often misinterpreted message of grace, I always go back to the Gospels of Jesus Christ. You can't go wrong when it's written in red. When we accept Jesus as our Lord and Savior, we are born again, but not yet saved. Matthew 10:22 says, "*But he that endureth to the end shall be saved.*" The finished work of Jesus on the cross was when His earthly mission was fulfilled. Our mission is only beginning. Those who ascribe to the doctrine that being born again equals salvation often see no deliverances, healings, or true salvation within their congregation. Being saved and being born again are two different things. John 3:7 says, "*Marvel not that I said unto thee, Ye must be born again.*" "Born" is translated from the Greek word **anagennao**, which means "to be begat" or "bear again."

To be born again means to start over, as from the beginning. This has to do with time. Grace also has to do with time. When we accept Jesus as our Savior from sin, our time clock starts over. We get a brand new start to get right with God.

If Jesus work on the cross is indeed finished, why do so many born again Christians still sin? Philippians 2:12 tells us, "*Wherefore, my beloved, as ye have always obeyed, not as in my presence only, but now much more in my absence, **work out your own salvation** with **fear** and **trembling**"* (emphasis added). Paul wrote this letter to the New Testament church in Philippi. He told them that salvation was, a work in progress. So, where do we get the "once saved always saved" doctrine along with the finished work of the cross? Notice that the way to salvation is marked with fear and trembling, not grace! People confuse God's mercy with His grace. Hebrews discusses this in depth.

Hebrews 10:28 says "*He that **despised Moses' law** died without **mercy** under two or three witnesses*" (emphasis added). This scripture uses the word **mercy**, not **grace.** The word "mercy" refers to the compassion and sympathy God has for us. The next verse, Hebrews 10:29, states, "*Of **how much worse punishment,** do you suppose, will he be thought worthy **who has trampled the Son of God underfoot,** counted the **blood of the covenant** by which he was sanctified a common thing, and **insulted the Spirit of grace**?*" (NKJV, emphasis added). Hebrews 10:28 explains that there was no mercy under the Law of Moses. If you

146

sinned, you died. No questions asked. But verse twenty nine tells us how much worse the punishment will be for a new covenant believer who insults the Spirit of grace. If you are continually late for work after your boss has given you many grace periods, you will be written up and eventually fired.

Hebrews 10:26 says, "*For if we sin willfully after that we have received the knowledge of the truth, there remaineth no more sacrifice for sins*" (emphasis added). Once we have accepted Jesus as our Savoir from sin, we cannot turn back to what we've been delivered from. Once you know the truth, sinning willfully brings judgment. Hebrews 6:6 says, "*If they shall fall away, to renew them again unto repentance; seeing they crucify to themselves the Son of God [Jesus], and put Him to an open shame*" (emphasis added). This is one of my favorite verses in the Bible. It states that, we are crucifying Jesus and putting him to shame all over again when we fall back into sin. Every time we sin and repent, Jesus has to be spat upon, beaten, whipped, crucified, and stabbed in His side all over again.

The work of the cross isn't finished. Jesus remains in heaven with his pierced hands, feet, and sides. He doesn't get His fully glorified body until we receive ours during the rapture. His body is still being crucified on the earth daily. Romans 8:17 says, "*And if children, then heirs; heirs of God, and joint-heirs with Christ; if so be that we suffer with him, that we may be also glorified together*" (emphasis added).

We are joint heirs, with Jesus, to the promise of glory. We are equal. If we suffer crucifying the flesh and picking up our crosses daily through denying self, then we will receive a glorified body with Him. The sacrificing will finally be over in that day. This Scripture uses the future tense, outlining what God promises us if we continue in the daily routine of killing the flesh and walking in the Spirit. I would like to enlighten those who misinterpret grace with a New Testament Bible verse. Romans 6:22–23 says, "*But now being **made free from sin**, and become servants to God, ye have your **fruit unto holiness**, and the end everlasting life. For the **wages of sin is death**; but the **gift of God is eternal life** through Jesus Christ our Lord*" (emphasis added). Stop paying for your death with the currency of sin, and bear the fruit of holiness. Make Jesus your Lord. Remember, if He is not Lord of all the parts of your life, then He is not Lord of your life at all. The purpose of this chapter was not to convert people to legalism or Judaism, but to fulfill the righteousness of the law of God through His grace. T.A.P.!

—⁓—

I pray right now in the name of Jesus Christ, Lord, let your people understand your definitions of grace and mercy. Give them a holy fear of you, Lord, and grant them extensions on the grace periods you set forth after your resurrection. Lord, we know you are merciful, but you are also a holy judge. May conviction of the Spirit of God fall upon everyone who reads this chapter and prayer. In Jesus name!

Chapter 9

The Ezekiel Warning

Ezekiel was a priest and a prophet that God used during the dark days of Judah's seventy year captivity in Babylon. Ezekiel's prophecies, parables, signs, and symbols dramatized and delivered God's message to His exalted people. The Israelites were dry bones in the sun, but God would soon reassemble them and breathe life back into the nation. The Hebrew name for Ezekiel is "Yechezqel, meaning "God strengthens" or "strengthened by God." Ezekiel's warning is located in Ezekiel 16:49 which says: "*Behold, this was the iniquity of thy sister Sodom, pride, fullness of bread, and abundance of idleness was in her and in her daughters, neither did she strengthen the hand of the poor and needy.*"

Iniquity

Ezekiel first addresses "*the iniquity of thy sister Sodom.*" "Iniquity" in this passage is translated from the Hebrew word **avon**, which means "moral evil," "perversity," "depravity," or "guilt." In iniquity, there is no perception of right versus wrong, or sense of moral value. Intentional sinning leaves everything in disarray. As Glenda Jackson says, it can be like having one foot in the world and the other in God.

149

Iniquity has everything to do with your own personal character and behavior and nothing to do with the influence of demonic forces. As I mentioned previously, the devil accuses the brethren because the brethren keep accusing him. Iniquity is self-willed and self-afflicted. It is the main cause of the trials, tribulations, poverty, and illness we encounter in life.

Psalm 103:2–3 says, "*Bless the LORD, O my soul, and forget not all his benefits: Who forgiveth all thine iniquities; who healeth all thy diseases*" (emphasis added). Look at the prophetic order: once iniquity is forgiven, healing takes place. This prophetic pattern also shows up in one of Isaiah's Old Testament prophecies. He describes the Messiah's atonement for the world in Isaiah 53:5: "*But he was wounded for our transgression, he was bruised for our iniquities: the chastisement of our peace was upon him; and with his stripes we are healed*" (emphasis added).

Do you see the prophetic pattern again? Jesus was touched for our transgressions and iniquities first, then the healing by His stripes took place. Both writers are clear on this point. The transgressions and iniquities are ours, not the devil's. "Transgression" is rebellion. In Hebrew, it is the word *pasha*, which means "to break away from authority." The Greek word *parabasis* is translated as "transgression," meaning "to disregard or violate a command." Jesus said in John 14:15, "*If ye love me, keep my commandments.*" If you are violating the Lord's commandments and living in iniquity you don't love God.

Let's address another point in Isaiah 53:5, which says, "*The chastisement of our peace was upon him*" (emphasis added). Chastisement must take place in order for us to receive peace. "Chastisement" here is translated from the Hebrew word *mocerowth*, stemming from a word that means "to chastise, correct, and instruct." The burden of correcting the world in a backwards religious society

150

was laid upon Jesus. The scribes and Pharisees plotted to kill Him because they could not handle His correction.

If the Lord brought correction to the church and to the children of God then, what makes us think He would not do it now? Perhaps our iniquity has blinded us to the truth of His Word. In 2 Corinthians 4:3–4, Paul tells us: "*But if our gospel be hid, it is hid to them that are lost: In whom the god of this world hath blinded the minds of them which believe not.*" A lost person is a believer who has gone astray. Their minds are of the world, so the god of this world can blind their minds. Iniquity reveals one's carnality and worldliness. *If you're a friend of the world, you're an enemy to God* (James 4:4). Isaiah 53:5 tells us what happens when iniquity is taken care of, "*With his stripes we are healed.*" Healing virtue is administered when iniquity is destroyed.

Pride

Now that we understand what iniquity is, and the seriousness of it, we can look at the rest of the Ezekiel warning. The warning outlines specific iniquities. Pride is first on the list. Pride is dangerous because it's hard to detect in one's self. The word translated as "pride in Ezekiel 16:49 is ***ga'own,*** meaning "arrogance." In the Greek, "pride" is ***typhoo***, which means "to be high-minded or inflated with self-conceit." Self-conceit is an exaggerated opinion of one's self, vanity, or pridefullness.

If you take the letters *e* and *p* away from the word **"*pride*"**, you get the word "**rid**." Pride will "**rid**" you of the Lord's blessings. Take away just the letter *p* from the word ***pride***, and you get the word "***ride***". Pride takes you on a journey of mayhem and destruction that you won't notice until it's too late. Pride is the main element in sin that keeps people from coming to Christ and serving him. Proverbs

16:18 tells us, *"Pride goeth before destruction, and a haughty spirit before a fall."* Pride and a haughty spirit are co-laborers in the destruction and fall of mankind. "Haughty" is translated from the Hebrew word **gobahh**, meaning "high or height; a place to fall from."

Since pride and haughtiness caused our fall, let's refer to the greatest fall of all and see if there are any instances of pride in the Scripture.

Let's go to Genesis 3:5-6:

> *For God doth know that in the day ye eat thereof, then your eyes shall be opened, and* ***ye shall be as gods****, knowing good and evil. And when the woman saw that the tree was good for food, and that it was pleasant to the eyes, and a tree to be desired to **make one wise**, she took of the fruit thereof, and did eat, and gave also unto her husband with her; and he did eat.* [Emphasis added.]

First, the serpent (satan) told Eve that *"Ye shall be as gods,"* and sowed the seed of pride within her. This same seed of pride took root in satan before he fell, making him think he could rise above God Almighty (Isaiah 14:14). In Genesis 3:6, we see the seed of pride growing. It states, *"And when the woman saw that the tree was good for food, and that it was pleasant to the eyes, and **a tree to be desired to make one wise**"* (emphasis added). Eve wanted to be as wise as God. Sometimes, pursuing knowledge and wisdom too heavily can bring on a prideful spirit.

In the wrong hands, revelation can bring disaster. Through Eve's actions, and the weakness of Adam, mankind lost their position of authority in the earth realm. The limitations of uncovered human beings emerged. When pride causes you to fall, your limitations are laid bare, and your fall becomes your reality.

Fullness of Food

Ezekiel 16:49 lists the "*fullness of bread*" as the next iniquity. The first sin mankind committed was eating a forbidden food. One of the United States' main issues is the fullness of food. The country has one of the highest obesity rates in the world. The body of Christ suffers from a spirit of gluttony, especially in this consuming culture. We eat immoderately and we rarely fast. As a result, our sensitivity to the Spirit and our ability to hear God is hindered.

Throughout the Bible, when a country falls away from God, the Lord spares the people when they fast, repent, and turn from their wicked ways. Food is meant for nourishing the body, not for over indulging. The Lord wants us to enjoy food, However, He doesn't want us to destroy our bodies by overeating. This is the warning in Philippians 3:19: " *Whose end is destruction, **whose God is their belly**, and whose glory is in their shame, who mind earthly things.*" When we overeat we are making our belly's our god.

Idleness

The next iniquity on Ezekiel's list is an "*abundance of idleness*" (16:49). The word idle means "lazy," "useless," "inactive" or "unemployed," "slow speed," or "out of gear." When we are idle, we slow the flow of our blessings. We fall out of gear and out of tune with God, and our journey comes to a standstill. The motion of the Spirit comes to a halt. Idle time is the devil's workshop, and he is working overtime to plague us with the spirit of distraction. The word "idle" in Greek is **argos**, which means "useless" or "barren." When we're idle, we're useless and unproductive. Idleness will abort in the natural realm the spiritual visions, dreams, and gifts that God gives you. Don't let idleness keep you from being fruitful.

The Poor

The last warning, which we read in Ezekiel 16:49, says "*Neither did she strengthen the hand of the poor and needy.*" Most people know that the poor need to be fed. Even non-Christian organizations understand this concept. However, if we merely feed the poor, we are not strengthening them. Instead we are making them codependent. The scripture said to strengthen the hand of the poor, not just feed them. How do we strengthen the poor? We can empower them through education, job opportunities, and treating them as first class citizens.

The Bible clearly states in Proverbs 14:20: "*The **poor is hated** even of his own neighbour: but **the rich hath many friends**"* (emphasis added). We must treat the poor and needy with the same respect and honor as a rich person. Touching the poor is first on the Holy Spirit's priority list when He anoints you. Jesus said in Luke 4:18: "*The Spirit of the Lord is upon me, because **he hath anointed me to preach the gospel to the poor**"* (emphasis added). The Spirit of the Lord anointed Jesus so he could preach to the poor. It was never God's intention for His people to be poor.

Poverty is a sin from the devil. Proverbs 10:15 says, "*The rich man's wealth is his strong city: the **destruction of the poor is their poverty**"* (emphasis added). Poverty brings destruction. It is never a good thing.

Judgment will come to both the poor and those who wrong the poor. God loves the poor. Isaiah 11:4 tells us, "*But with righteousness shall he judge the poor.*" The poor will be judge with righteousness. What you do in this life counts in the afterlife. Jesus says in Revelation 22:12, "*And behold, I come quickly; and my reward is with me, to give every man according as his work shall be.*" Your reward in heaven will be given according to the labor you did on earth. We must help the poor and needy, and they must also be willing to help themselves.

God will bless the hands that strengthen the hands of the poor. The Lord promises in Proverbs 28:27, *"He that giveth unto the poor shall not lack: but he that hideth his eyes shall have many a curse."* Your spiritual and financial lack will be taken away when you give to the poor. Furthermore, giving to the poor is a command, not a suggestion. When you have the power to supply a need and you don't, destruction will come to your own situations. This is what Ezekiel was trying to warn the people about. There are consequences for failing to aid the poor. If we have not received the full blessing of God's promises, we may want to consider if we are failing to help those in need. Giving to the poor makes you perfect in God's eyes, and it accesses the currency of heaven. Let's look at the rich, young ruler.

Matthew 19:16–22 tells the whole story. Verse twenty one says, *"Jesus said unto him, **If thou wilt be perfect**, go and sell all that thou hast, and **give to the poor**, and **thou shalt have treasure in heaven**: and come and follow me"* (emphasis added). The young ruler had already kept the commandments since birth, but it was through the principles of giving to the poor, that he would store up treasures in heaven and be perfected in God's sight. Even though the young ruler had earthly treasure, he didn't have heavenly treasure. Heavenly treasure is not just for the life beyond, it also helps one perform supernatural exploits in the earthly realm.

In Philippians 4:19, Paul says, *"But my **God shall supply all your needs** according to **his riches in glory** by Christ Jesus"* (emphasis added). God's riches and treasures are in His heavenly realms ready to be purposed towards our earthly needs. Remember, treasure in heaven accesses heaven's currency onto earth. For example, Jesus accessed his heavenly account to multiply the two fishes and five loaves to feed the five thousand (John 6:1–6).

Before Paul stated that God would supply our needs through Jesus riches and glory, he first asked for an earthly offering in order to access that heavenly blessing.

In Philippians 4:17 he says, "*Not because I desire a gift: but I desire fruit that **may abound to your account**.*" (emphasis added). Paul was saying that, through earthly giving, those in need could withdraw Kingdom currency from heaven.

But, what do you have in your account? Is your account in the negative, or is it thriving? Are you living off heaven's 1,000 percent interest? The banking system of heaven is in your favor when you give to the poor. The Scripture says in Proverbs 19:17, "*He that **hath pity upon the poor lendeth unto the Lord**; and that which **he hath given will pay him again**"* (emphasis added). When you have pity on the poor, you give out of compassion. The word pity means "a feeling of compassion or sorrow for another's misfortune." Don't give to the poor for the sake of mere principles or works, but give out of compassion. Compassion accesses the blessings. The scripture says that when you do this, you lend to the Lord.

Do you know anyone who can say that they lend money to the Lord? According to Proverbs 22:7, "*The borrower is servant to the lender.*" So when you lend to God by giving to the poor, God, according to His Word, is obligated to serve you. During this time, you have heaven at your disposal. Last but not least, Proverbs 19:17 tells us that what you have given will be paid back with interest. Not only do you get to access heaven, but you also get reimbursed for your initial investment with even more added on.

In the midst of the Ezekiel warning, we can find a silver lining if we T.A.P. through the principle of removing sin from our midst and destroying the prideful spirit. We must not over indulge with our eating, and we should fast often. We also need to avoid idleness and stay busy in the Lord. Finally, we must strengthen the poor through seed sowing, education, revelation, and compassion for their needs.

—⁊⁊⁊—

I pray, in the name of Jesus, that every person who reads this chapter and prays will take heed of the Ezekiel warning. Turn from your wicked ways, follow the instruction, and remove any corruption that would bring destruction. I release the power of the blessing upon you. I pray you be clothed in a mantle of righteousness and holy love for your neighbor. May the Lord of peace keep you on the right path. We seal this prayer with the blood of Jesus. Amen. T.A.P.

Chapter 10
Tips to T.A.P.

Repentance

While seeking revelation in the glory realm of the Lord, I received this first tip. I repent before every service I attend. That way, I'm more sensitive to receiving from the Lord. 2 Timothy 2:21 says: "*If a man therefore purges [purifies] himself from these, he shall be a vessel unto honour, sanctified, and meet [ready] for the master's use, and prepared unto every good work*" (emphasis added). Through repentance, I make myself ready for the master's use, and it prepares me for every good work. The Holy Spirit told me that "tip" means: "The Important Principles." I am not just giving you anointed principles, but also the most important ones. And repentance is the first and foremost among all T.I.P.'s to T.A.P.

Seek God's Presence

Let's move on to the second tip. Discern where the glory is most present and be there. You must become a glory chaser. Wherever the cloud is, you must be under it. Don't be without His presence. Develop the mindset that, if the presence is not there, you won't be there. Exodus 33:15 confirms this: "*And he said unto him, If thy presence go not with me, carry us not up hence.*" Don't take a title, job, or a position in the church without confirmation from the Holy Spirit. Likewise, don't enter into a relationship unless the assignment is confirmed with the tangible manifestation of God's presence. A lack of His presence is a lack of His protection. Once again, Job 2:7 says: "*So went Satan forth from the presence of LORD, and smote Job with sore boils from the sole of his foot unto his crown.*" The devil wasn't able to touch Job's body until he left the presence of God. You must become a presence seeker.

Some say it's not about a "feeling." I say, how would you know God is there without sensing the manifestation of His presence through the five senses of the spirit? Humans experience physical reality through the five physical senses: taste, touch, smell, sight, and hearing. When it comes to discerning God's presence, the same principle exists in the spiritual realm. Remember without His presence you can't receive His presents.

Give to Ministers

The third tip is this: sow something into the life of the anointed vessel (minister) that God is using to impart spiritual gifts unto you. Paul states clearly in 1 Corinthians 9:11: "*If we have sown unto you spiritual things, is it a great thing if we shall reap your material things?*" We allow the enemy to rob us of our full inheritance when we approach giving to the men or women of God with a double mind. Giving to ministers is one of the ways we receive our full blessings from God.

Leviticus 23:20 tells us: "*And the priest shall wave them with the bread of the firstfruits for a wave offering before the LORD, with the two lambs: they shall be holy to the LORD for the priest*" (emphasis added). Offerings are holy to God, but they belong to the priest. There isn't a spaceship big enough to travel to Heaven and deliver your tithes and offerings to God, it still must be distributed through a man.

When we bless the men and women of God, the Lord imparts things of the spiritual realm. It's our duty to bless them with our possessions. Luke 8:2–3 tells us about

> *"certain women, which had been healed of evil spirits and infirmities, Mary called Magdalene, out of whom went seven devils, And Joanna the wife of Chuza Herod's steward, and Susanna, and many others, which **ministered unto him of their substance.***"* [Emphasis added.]

Jesus allowed people to sow into His life and ministry as these grateful women did. When Jesus delivered the women from their evil spirits and diseases, they responded by giving him offerings. When someone takes the time to minister to us, we must minister back with our material possessions.

Let Paul's words in 2 Corinthians 11:7–8 be clarified: "***Did I commit sin** in humbling myself **that you might be exalted**, because **I preached the gospel of God** to you **free of charge**? I **robbed other churches, taking wages** from them to **minister to you**"* (emphasis added). Paul poses a question: "Have I sinned by working myself and receiving from (robbing) other churches so I wouldn't have to take anything from you Corinthians?" "Robbed" in this passage is translated as the word ***sulao,*** which means "to take from" or "to take away," in the Greek. Though he had not taken money from them, he still received from other churches abroad.

A few verses later, in 2 Corinthians 11:11, Paul says, "*Wherefore? because I love you not? God knoweth.*" Paul was concerned that taking the Corinthian church's money would send a signal that he didn't love them. But, he was confident of his motives, and he trusted God to convict him of any wrong thinking. Paul knew that receiving offerings would give his enemies ammunition to slander him and accuse him of greed. There was a very real danger that the spread of the Gospel would be hindered in the region because of that reason. However, Paul also knew by not receiving an offering from them, also hindered them from receiving from the Lord. He stated; *I preached the gospel of God to you free of charge...*If we as ministers pay the price to receive the anointing, you must pay a price to receive it as well. The anointing cost.

Give to the anointed vessels, and allow them to give to you, so you don't rob those who give or hinder those who haven't given.

Inhale the Spirit

Here's the fourth tip: learn to inhale the atmosphere. One of the definitions of atmosphere is "a predominant mood or feeling." When God's presence is in the atmosphere, using breathing techniques can allow His presence to better enter our systems. This theory doesn't have much scriptural backing, but John 20:22 says, "*And when he had said this, **he breathed on them**, and saith unto them, **Receive ye the Holy Ghost**"* (emphasis added). Every time I inhale the Spirit, I receive a stronger sense of God's glory.

The most frequent translation of spirit" is from the Hebrew word ***ruwach***, which means "breath," "wind," "inspiration," or "exhalation." Thus, the spirit realm has something to do with breathing and exhaling. When we inhale and exhale deeply in a meeting, we receive, or take in, the spirit of that meeting. Often, yawning is contagious, and just like yawning the spirit is contagious as well, once you release it in the atmosphere everyone can catch it. Satan may be the prince of the air, but God is the creator of it. Genesis 2:7 says, "*And the LORD God formed man of the dust of the ground, and **breathed into his nostrils** the **breath of life**; and man became a **living soul**"* (emphasis added). God gave life by blowing the breath of His Spirit into the nostrils of man. Therefore, when we need a fresh word or a fresh anointing, breathing God's breath, or Spirit, will give us new life just as it was at the beginning. T.A.P.!

Live Sacrificially

This fifth principle is one of the most important tips to T.A.P. In fact, it sums up the whole book. The principle I speak of is the principle of sacrificial living. Throughout the Old Testament, and even in the New Testament, God always answered the people when sacrifices were made. After The Fall and before the Law of Moses, sacrifices were primarily "gifts", offered to God as a way of connecting with Him. The system of sacrifices was set up during the Mosaic period. Sacrifices became functions of receiving forgiveness of sin and dedicating of the giving of gifts. Still, the main purpose of sacrifices was to bring right relationship and connection between man and God. Jesus became the ultimate sacrifice for forgiveness. He restored the relationship between the Father and all men who received him. This is clearly put forth in Hebrews 9.

In Revelation 5:12 we read: "*Worthy is the **Lamb that was slain** to receive power, and riches, and wisdom, and strength, and honour, and glory, and blessing*" (emphasis added). The Book of Revelation frequently refers to Jesus as "the Lamb." He is the sacrifice used to make atonement and amends for sins. Jesus was the greatest sacrificial Lamb there ever was. Jesus also lived a sacrificial lifestyle, and He wants us to continue this practice. In Matthew 16:24; Jesus clearly states this important principle: "*If any man will come after me, let him deny himself, and take up his cross and, follow me.*" Denying oneself is the initial step. Denying yourself means refusing to partake in something you desire. This process of denial makes you *selfless,* not *selfish.* You channel your focus towards others when you deny yourself.

When you do this, you will access the ultimate power of love. You must sacrifice yourself for others in order to obtain the power of love. Jesus demonstrated this love on the cross. He tells us in John 15:13, "*Greater love hath no man than this, that a man lay down his life for his friends.*" You haven't mastered the love walk until you are willing to lay down your life for others. Jesus embraced the cross. We must follow the same pattern. Jesus tells us in Matthew 16:24 to deny ourselves, take up our crosses, and follow Him. You must take up your cross, not run from it. One day the Holy Spirit told me, "***If I have to drag you to the cross, it means you don't want to be crucified.*** *You don't want to die to the flesh.*"

Romans 12:1 tells us, "*I beseech you therefore brethren, by the mercies of God, that* ***ye present your bodies as a living sacrifice****, holy, acceptable unto God, which is* ***your reasonable service.***"(emphasis added). The sacrifice of the body, or the flesh, refers to fasting, praying, and denying worldly pleasures. A sacrificial lifestyle is our reasonable duty.

The Lord doesn't want us to go overboard with a sacrificial lifestyle, but He wants us to make it a habit and not a hobby. This is the least we can and should do. Don't break this habit, because it will bring you extraordinary benefits. Revelation 5:12 says, "*The* ***Lamb that was slain*** *to* ***receive power****, and* ***riches****, and* ***wisdom****, and* ***strength****, and* ***honour****, and* ***glory*** *and* ***blessing***" (emphasis added).

This scripture shows us the benefits of being a sacrificial lamb. It says that "***the Lamb that was slain to receive***". You can't receive power, riches, wisdom, strength, honor, glory, and blessings from the Lord unless you're a sacrificial lamb. In John 21:15 the Lamb, Jesus, says, "*Saith to Simon Peter, Simon, son of Jonas, lovest thou me more than these? He saith unto him, Yea, Lord; thou knowest that I love thee, He saith unto him,* ***Feed my lambs***" (emphasis added). Jesus is speaking of His followers (us) as lambs, sacrificial beings for God.

Paul quotes Psalm 44:22 in Romans 8:36: "*As it is written, For thy sake **we are killed all the day long**; we are accounted as **sheep for the slaughter**"* (emphasis added). Paul is describing the war between the flesh and spirit. We must live sacrificial lifestyles on a daily basis and be "*killed all the daylong*". We must deny our flesh so our spirit man can dominate our lives. Once again, this must be a habit and not just a hobby.

Paul speaks of self-sacrifice again in 1 Corinthians 15:31: "*I protest by your rejoicing which I have in Christ Jesus our Lord, **I die daily**"* (emphasis added). We must die daily to our fleshly desires and deny ourselves. If we do not wake up with the funeral of the flesh on our minds, then we will perish physically and spiritually. Every day, I wake up with a holy suicidal spirit that wants to kill the flesh of Shawn Morris the man, so that the prophet in me can live. Cut away the layers of flesh that deny you access to the spirit realm.

We must kill the flesh before it kills us. It's survival of the fittest, kill or be killed. Romans 8:13 tells us, "*For if ye **live after the flesh, ye shall die**: but if ye through the Spirit do **mortify the deeds of the body**, ye shall live*" (emphasis added). Mortify means "to destroy strength or vitality" or "to deny self." We need to destroy the strength of the flesh to prevent strongholds from arising. When we live sacrificially by dwelling in the spirit, and killing the flesh, we can regain the keys that unlock the heavens.

We must remember that the lust of the flesh itself is the problem, not us.

We don't own those fleshly desires and thoughts, our fleshly, sinful nature does. The enemy can't attack you if he has nothing to latch onto. We have access to the Helper when we deny and remove the flesh. Let's T.A.P. through sacrificial living.

The last and most important key to sacrificial living is, maintaining a broken spirit. This is more than a mere principle. All of God's children need to practice this lifestyle. There are several meanings of the word broken. One is the Hebrew word **atsam**, which means "to be made powerful or numerous." When you're broken before the Lord, you are being made powerful.

Let's look at the importance of being broken in Scripture. Psalm 51:17 reads, "*The sacrifices of God are a broken spirit: a broken and contrite heart, O God, thou wilt not despise.*" A broken spirit is the key to revival. We want miracles, signs, and wonders, but God wants a broken spirit. We can fast and give our best financial offerings, but the Lord is looking for a broken spirit above all. All over the world, churches and ministries hold meetings and receive healings and breakthroughs for their own personal gain. However, we rarely see broken people approaching the altar and seeking the Lord. Manifestations are for our benefit, but a broken spirit is for God's benefit.

When we implement this principle, we will unlock spiritual blessings. God promises us this result. Psalm 51:19 says: "*Then shalt thou be pleased with the sacrifices of righteousness, with burnt offering and whole burnt offering: then shall they offer bullocks upon thine alter.*" Once we offer a broken spirit up to God, He will honor the rest of our sacrifices. A study of past revivals and moves of God's Spirit will reveal a common ingredient. That ingredient, my friend, is a broken spirit.

Many people desire an infilling of the spirit, but not an outpouring. The Scriptures says, in Joel 2:12," "*Therefore also now, saith the Lord, turn ye even to me **with all your heart**, and with fasting, and with **weeping**, and with **mourning**.*" We must come before the Lord with all our heart. The Lord wants to deal with our heart issues. When we come before God with weeping and mourning, we can gain access to the throne room with ease. The weeping symbolizes our sorrow over our sins, and mourning represents the dying of the flesh. Whenever there is mourning, something is surely dying. We need to put ourselves on the altar of brokenness and come before the mercy seat of the Lord through sacrificial living. T.A.P.

Close Your Eyes to the Soulish Realm

The sixth tip: remove yourself from the soulish realm by closing your eyes. The eye is the organ of sight. In the Scriptures the **"eye"** is a frequent metaphor for spiritual perception and understanding. Psalm 19:28 tells how the Word of God enlightens the eyes. The eyes offer enlightened understanding that leads to growth and spiritual knowledge in Ephesians 1:18. The eye is also used as a metaphor for personal character. *A good man has a "bountiful eye"* according to Psalm 22:9. In Psalm 131:1, *the proud man has lofty (haughty) eyes.* The envious man has an evil eye, according to Matthew 20:15.

The eyes are the windows to the soul. When we shut those windows against the things of the world, we remove ourselves from the soulish realm. Even though the eye is one of the smallest areas in the body, it consists of many different parts. A picture is worth a thousand words. You aren't a camera, but you possess the ability to capture photographic moments with your eye. The eye is one of the main "digestive" tracts to the soulish realm. Nutrient or toxic material, whichever one enters first, gets into the soul through here. The ears are also a window to the soul. Whatever enters through seeing and hearing goes into the soul. The eyes and ears are the main gates that sin and evil try to breach.

Jesus said, *"And if thy **right eye offend** thee, pluck it out, and cast it from thee: for it is profitable for thee that one of thy members should perish, and not that **the whole body should be cast into hell**"* (Matthew 5:29, emphasis added). This Scripture shows us that the eye defiles the body and could even land us in hell. In 2 Corinthians 5:7 we read,

166

"*For we walk by faith, not by sight.*" We must learn to walk by faith in the spirit, and not by what our eyes see. When you're trying to T.A.P., close your eyes and shut yourself off from the world. Close the soulish window and enter into the supernatural.

Ask, Seek, Knock

The seventh tip: there are three steps to entering God's presence. These steps are the holy trinity of all the principles: **ask, seek, knock.** All three dimensions of entry into the glory realm are summed up in the first step of penetrating the spirit world, which is **ask**. One translation of the word *ask* is the Hebrew word *baquash*, which means "to search out" or "to strive after." When we begin to ask the Lord for something, we must use more than verbal gestures. We must have a striving and diligent attitude to be heard.

Most people don't like to strive for anything.

Even those who move in the glory realm love to emphasize resting in the Lord over striving. Resting in the Lord is important, but we must also remember that striving is necessary to enter into that rest. Hebrews 4:11 says: "*Let us labour therefore to enter into that rest.*" The "rest" doctrine has crippled the body of Christ and created believers who are too lazy to contend for the faith. The Bible even says in Philippians 3:14, "*I **press toward the mark** for the **prize of the high calling** of God in Christ Jesus.*" If we don't press forward, we will never see the prize of the high calling of God. We must build up our spiritual muscle by pressing forward in the natural. During Moses earthly ministry, there were times when God fought for the Israelites through His sovereign touch of glory. Then, there were times when the children of Israel had to fight for themselves in the physical realm while the Lord backed them up in the spiritual realm. Taking action in the asking realm gets God's attention.

The next step, or realm, is **seek**: I love this step because it requires a little more effort on our part. The majority of the world wants God to come running after them. They want Him to prove that He is real before they believe in or serve Him. But, God is not the predator He is the prey, that's why we must pray, so we may eat of Him. Jesus is the bread of life, and we must partake of Him in order to live forever (see John 6: 22–53). The Lord is a "player". I understand the nature of a player. A player does not chase after women. Women chase after him. Don't misunderstand what I am saying, ladies and gentlemen, I am not equating the Lord with a player. However, He has a similar approach to relationships. In Scripture, He says *"draw nigh to God, and he will draw nigh to you"* (James 4:8). God wants to be sought after. He wants to be chased. He won't move until we move. You woo God into an intimate conversation while you are in the seeking realm.

According to Proverbs 18:22, the husband may find the wife, but seeking is what prepares the bride for her husband. The wife must lure the husband with her beauty before she is chosen as a bride. Seeking the Lord in worship, prayer, fasting, and total obedience is the only way to get beautified. Many of us are believers, but not seekers. Mere belief in something or someone can't keep your faith intact. You have to seek out what you believe in. The faith of too many believers starts to waver after a time. Often, this happens because God doesn't answer a prayer in time, or because the cares of the world seem more real and tangible than God. This shaky faith is bred by a lack of seeking. After the asking realm is entered, the seeking realm becomes the most vital principle. In the seeking realm, you will learn the map to the Holy of Holies.

The final step in the holy trinity of principles is **knock**. The knocking realm opens the door to a new dimension in the spirit. Matthew 7:7 says, *"Ask, and it **shall be given** you; seek, and ye **shall find**; knock, and **it shall be opened** unto you"* (emphasis added). We may be given an answer after we ask for it, but that doesn't mean we possess it quite yet. Asking is the invitation to the treasure hunt. That's why the seeking level follows it.

Like I mentioned earlier, the seeking realm provides the map that we use to locate the treasure. It is knocking that finally opens up the door or treasure box that we find. Knocking is the final principle of entry needed to obtain the splendor of the riches of God's glory. God wants to bless His people, but we must follow these principles in order to gain access to the assets of His Kingdom. Here is an application of the knocking realm in Scripture: "*Then shalt thou call, and the Lord shall answer; thou shalt cry, and he shall say, Here I am*" (Isaiah 58:9, emphasis added).

When we ask God, He answers. When we cry out, He will say "here I am." If your child is calling your name from upstairs, you may answer, "What do you want?" Yet, you may decide not to move from where you are. However, if your child cries out or screams, you will drop what you're doing, rush to him or her, and say, "Here I am." Someone calls your phone, you may not answer right away. But if that certain someone keeps dialing your number, eventually you will pick up. And, if the situation is serious enough, you will say, "I'm on my way." That's what happens between the believer and God in the knocking realm.

The body of Christ needs to learn how to cry out to the Lord. Crying out is knocking on the door with repeated force. In the knocking realm, you gain God's undivided attention and forces His hand to aid you in your request. I often tell people as a joke, "Don't knock the knockers."

Once we apply all three of these steps ask, seek, and knock we will find ourselves living under an open heaven where nothing is impossible. T.A.P.

Be a Sin Hunter

The following tip is the most important one of all. You won't see the full measure of God's glory without it. No matter how much you ask, seek, and knock, without this tip, you will T.A.P. out. Therefore, you must become a sin hunter.

Sin means "to miss the mark," "to err," or "to make a mistake." Sin is the cancer to a Christian's lifespan on earth. Sin is anything in us that doesn't reflect God's holy character.

Adam and Eve committed the first sin on earth in the Garden. They followed their own wills and deliberately went against the instructions of God. However, sin was present in the universe long before satan (Lucifer) rebelled against God. In essence, sin is choosing to functioning independently of God.

The majority of our life issues stem from sin or ignorance. Sin is the culprit that prevents people from receiving or keeping their healing. Psalm 103:3 says to bless the Lord "*who forgiveth all thine iniquities; who healeth all thy diseases.*" Notice that the forgiveness of sin (iniquities) comes before the healing of diseases. You can't receive a full healing without the removal of sins.

Isaiah 53:5 tells us, "*But he was wounded for our transgressions, he was bruised for our iniquities: the chastisement of our peace was upon him; and with his stripes we are healed.*" Jesus was wounded, bruised, and chastised for our sins and transgressions. We have access to healing because He went through this pain and suffering for us to remove sin.

Transgressing is breaking away from, or rebelling against, the law. Your transgressions are not only offensive to people, but they are also a rebellion against the just authority of God. When we transgress, we grieve the Holy Spirit. Ephesians 4:30 tells us clearly, "*And grieve not the Holy Spirit of God, whereby ye are sealed unto the day of redemption*" (emphasis added). Usually, if someone is grieved, they leave. When we willfully grieve the Holy Spirit through sin, we remove His seal and allow evil spirits and infirmities to come in. This is counter-productive to the work of Jesus, who was made sick for our transgressions so we can be restored to the Lord's proper and just authority.

Our iniquities bruised and crush the Lord. "Bruised" in Isaiah 53:5 is translated from the Hebrew word *daka*, meaning "to be crushed or broken." "Iniquity" refers to wrongs and evil doing. Iniquities are always wrongs done on our part. The devil cannot be blamed. Every time we revive old sins that the shed blood of Jesus destroyed, we crush and break Jesus all over again. As I mentioned before, those who stay in their sins, "*crucify to themselves the Son of God afresh, and put him to an open shame*" (Hebrews 6:6).

People often overlook the prophetic word in Isaiah 53:5 concerning Jesus crucifixion: "*The chastisement of our peace was upon him*" (emphasis added). Chastisement disciplines our moral nature. Deuteronomy 11:2 tells us: "*And know ye this day: for I speak not with your children which have not known, and which have not seen the chastisement of the Lord your God, his greatness, his mighty hand, and his stretched out arm*" (emphasis added). Many want the love and grace of God without chastisement or correction. Yet, chastisement is one way the Lord cultivates our mind and moral fiber. Hebrews 12:11 reminds us: "*Now no chastening for the present seemeth to be joyous, but grievous nevertheless afterward it yielded the peaceable fruit of righteousness unto them which are exercised thereby*" (emphasis added). This is how you retrieve fruits of righteousness.

False teaching states that God's correction won't feel bad. If a sermon makes you feel uncomfortable, then it's not of God. But, Hebrews 12:11 refutes this teaching. When the Lord corrects, it

171

won't be joyous or pleasant. It will be painful. Some teach that we receive God's love through His grace, but it is really through His chastisement that we receive His true love. Hebrews 12:6 says, "*For **whom the Lord loveth he chasteneth**, and **scourgeth every son whom he receiveth**"* (emphasis added). This scripture goes even further, stating that the Lord scourges every son He accepts. Scourging is a horrible form of discipline and punishment, consisting of whipping or flogging with a whip.

The Greek word ***mastigoo***, translated as "scourgeth" in this verse, it can mean "a calamity or misfortune sent by God to discipline or punish." The Lord stated clearly that He would bring this chastisement on every son or daughter that He loves. To receive son-ship, you need chastisement. Further on the writer of Hebrews states: "*But if ye be **without chastisement**, whereof **all are partakers, then are ye bastards,** and **not sons**?"* (12:8, emphasis added). You're not a son or daughter of God without His chastisement. The writer also states that "*all are partakers*" of this correction. If you're a child of God and your not receiving correction in your Christian walk, then your considered a bastard and not a son or daughter according to scripture, because all are partakers of this correction. His correction brings protection, possession, and resurrection power, all of which are benefits of being His son. The encouraging thing about the chastisement of the Lord is that it will always bring peace to your life. Jesus is the prince of correction, just as much as he is the Prince of Peace. You can't obtain His peace without His correction.

When you become a sin hunter, you also become a peacekeeper. Matthew 5:9 says, "*Blessed are the peacemakers; for they shall be called the children of God.*" There is blessing in the principle of peacemaking. However, you can't be a peacemaker (from the Greek *eir nopoios*, meaning "pacific" or "loving peace") until you make peace with God first. Hunting sin and willingly receiving the

Lord's chastisement will help you make that peace. Remember the scripture says "**the chastisement of our peace** *was upon him.*" without chastisement we have no peace.

Peace is grossly misunderstood. Most think peace is a state devoid of problems. But, peace is complex concept with many definitions. The most popular definition in the Christian community comes from the Hebrew word **shalowm**, or shalom, which means "safety," "sound in body," "health," "tranquility," or completeness. Connect this definition of peace with the Hebrew word **qowl**, which means, "to call aloud or cry out." That's the kind of peacemakers we need to be: noisemakers for the Lord.

The quiet side of peace is represented by the Hebrew word **charash**, which means, "to be deaf or silent or concealed." You need this kind of peace when troubles break out in your life. However, having this kind of peace at the wrong time may conceal you from something the Lord is trying to reveal. We need to cry out loudly to spark up the faith in our lives.

In Matthew 10:34, Jesus says something that seemingly contradicts His character: "*Think not that I am come to send peace on earth: I came not to send peace, but a sword.*" How can the Prince of Peace bring a sword? Jesus isn't contradicting himself. When he says "sword", He is referring to His word. His word doesn't bring "**eirene**," which is the Greek word for tranquility, harmony, or rest. His Word challenges us to call out loud, to proclaim and cry out the good news of the Gospel, which will birth the peace that surpasses all understanding.

Your faith is being tested when your life is shaken. Jesus spoke to the sea and said, "*Peace be still*" (Mark 4:39). That "peace" was translated from the Greek word **siopao**, which means "to calm down and be quiet." Jesus told the noisy (peace) and thunderous sea to

173

hush. He used the storm to test the disciples' faith. He use peace to bring peace. He knew the tempest wouldn't hurt them. Instead, it would teach them how to receive peace. Jesus, who already had that shalom peace slept while the disciples lost their composure. Jesus wanted his followers to have the same inner control. If you can't calm the storm inside, you won't be able to silence the one that rages around you. Peace must permeate every area of your life.

Isaiah 53:5: "*With his stripes we are healed.*" When we become sin hunters by removing and destroying transgressions and iniquities, we must willingly accept the chastisement of the Lord so we can have peace. We must follow the biblical order so we can receive the full measure of God's presence and blessings. Then, we will finally be healed. So, let us T.A.P. through these "tips" to T.A.P!

—ᴍ—

I pray, in the name of Jesus Christ, that everyone receives revelation through the principles explained in this book. May the glory and power of God touch each individual who reads this. Bodies be healed right now in the mighty name of Jesus. Creative miracles, manifest. And finally, may the impartation to move in the miraculous, be released now! In Jesus name, it is done.

T.A.P.

Contact The Author

Email me at:
Prophet@shawnmorris.org,
and visit www.shawnmorris.org

For booking

Contact us at 281-818-6982.

Send all donation and tax deductible gifts to

P.O. Box 1802
Alief, Texas 77411

About The Author

Shawn Morris is a dynamic and anointed minister of the Gospel. He operates in a remarkable anointing that includes prophecy, healing, miracles, signs, and wonders. He is known as one of the most accurate prophets in the land, and he is a mentor to hundreds of pastors and ministries across the world. He is also the president and founder of Shawn Morris International Ministries in Houston Texas. As an international evangelist, Prophet Morris, along with his wife Tora, has led thousands to Christ and been the catalyst of small town revivals across the country. His methods of ministering in the glory of God have had a profound effect on thousands of people across the world. He and his wife's hearts for revival have inspired thousands across the country to contend for a higher calling in Christ. His goal is to empower the body of Christ to move into its full inheritance and identity. Prophet Morris resides in Houston Texas, with his wife and children.

CPSIA information can be obtained at www.ICGtesting.com
Printed in the USA
LVOW13s1956040814

397458LV00027B/1138/P